Goebel

Figurines
Designed By

Rocky Rockholt

4880 Lower Valley Road, Atglen, PA 19310 USA

This book has been researched and written to serve as a guide to Charlot Byj's works as produced by W. Goebel Porzellanfabrik, Germany.

I solicit your comments, questions, corrections and correspondence. No work is ever complete as there are always new discoveries to be made. Please write or contact me: Rocky Rockholt, 2678 Sumac Ridge, White Bear Lake, MN 55110-5646. Tel/fax 651-777-9000 or email at rockyrockholt@email.msn.com.

Designed by John P. Cheek
Type set in Korinna BT/Korinna BT

ISBN: 0-7643-1300-2
Printed in China
1 2 3 4

Published by Schiffer Publishing Ltd.
4880 Lower Valley Road
Atglen, PA 19310
Phone: (610) 593-1777; Fax: (610) 593-2002
E-mail: Schifferbk@aol.com
Please visit our web site catalog at
www.schifferbooks.com
We are always looking for people to write books on new and related subjects. If you have an idea for a book please contact us at the above address.

This book may be purchased from the publisher.
Include $3.95 for shipping.
Please try your bookstore first.
You may write for a free catalog.

In Europe, Schiffer books are distributed by
Bushwood Books
6 Marksbury Ave.
Kew Gardens
Surrey TW9 4JF England
Phone: 44 (0) 20 8392-8585; Fax: 44 (0) 20 8392-9876
E-mail: Bushwd@aol.com
Free postage in the U.K., Europe; air mail at cost.

DEDICATION

This book is dedicated to my wonderful redheaded wife, best friend and enabler, Marilyn. She was the first Redhead in my collection. She began the collection many years ago and together we have found joy and pleasure in collecting those cute little rascals designed by Charlot Byj.

Thank you, Marilyn, for being you!

CONTENTS

ACKNOWLEDGEMENTS

No book would be complete without acknowledgements to people who have contributed in some manner to that book. This could be information or advice, encouraging me to proceed, allowing me to photograph figurines from their collection, checking their own collection for painting variations or directing me to other collectors that shared an interest in the items designed by Charlot Byj.

These folks are listed here and in no particular order. To each of you, I truly appreciate your help and say "Thank You"! Sue Beranek, Gwen McCamley, Al and Marge Frecker, Jack Tysk, Jack and Joanne Brey, Pat Arbenz, Phyllis Cloughsey, Steve Cordes, Hubert McHugh, Mrs. Charles Morgan, Linda Nothnagel, Don Steward and many who have asked to be nameless.

Naturally, I must also give a hardy "Thank You" to the wonderful folks at Goebel - both domestic and in Germany. Your assistance and cooperation has been invaluable!

Charlot Byj's Redheads

So often the question has been asked, "Who are these fun little characters and where did they get their names?" This question can best be answered by Charlot Byj herself in a poem that she wrote to provide their identification. This information is from *Hummelwerk Messenger,* Volume 9, Number 2, November 1981.

Collectors who wrote - please note:

"My Roots"
by a Redhead

Here and now finally..
I reveal all... the real me
Just a devil-may-care...
Right on REDHEAD - Shabby
O'Hair
Do Redheads hatch...
..in a tomato patch?
Nein! Nein!
We come from a fine greeting card
line
(All red-in-the-thatch, natch.)

Sinclair N. O'Hair
is mon pere..
M'Lady O'Hair
is ma mere..
Raggy Muffin is my petite GAL
PAL

Stuffy Duffy's the
great guy who lives nearby..

Do we have class?
As you can see
We've even got a family tree...
And a coat of arms
(Designed by me!)
Waggy, my fun-lovin' pup,
is holding our motto:
YNNUF EDIS PU
"FUNNY SIDE UP" spelled
backwards.
Hope this enlightens you..
Your debonair,
glad that you care
Smiling Redhead
Shabby O'Hair.

This fun loving approach, as illustrated by the "family tree," has made each of these wonderful characters a favorite for collectors worldwide.

A BRIEF BIOGRAPHY OF CHARLOT BYJ

Charlot Byj's (pronounced Bye) love of children is very visible in all the works that she created. Her field of art was a broad one including the creation of the redheaded children that brought her to the attention of Franz Goebel of the Goebel Company in the mid 1940s.

She was born September 28, 1920, in Kingston, Pennsylvania, the fourth of four daughters, to John and Sophia Byj who were of Polish decent. Her early years followed the pattern of those of most other American girls of that period. She attended grammar school in Kingston, where she discovered her love of drawing at a very early age. With her first box of crayons, she freely decorated the book covers of each new batch of school tablets that were distributed monthly. In addition, she conducted a little business of made-to-order cut-out dolls complete with elaborate wardrobes, for her classmates.

In high school, she studied shorthand, typing, and book keeping, and is reputed to have hated every minute of it. After school, it was another world completely, as she designed covers and cartoons as well as writing humorous articles for the school magazine, the "Kingstonian." Art was her real world and what she really wanted to do for her life's vocation. She graduated from high school at the early age of 15.

Charlot's parents told her she could attend art college for one year, and if it didn't work out she could change to another college. It is reported that "she absolutely loved it" and kept receiving scholarships, so she was able to complete her training at the Philadelphia Museum School of Art, where she graduated after four years on a partial scholarship. While attending the Philadelphia Museum art school, she lived at Crozier Hall—a YWCA residence. The school had no dormitory at that time. She is said to have covered her YWCA room walls with Hummel cards wishing that she could work in that manner.

After graduation from art school she found it very difficult to find the type of work for which she longed so desperately. She took freelance assignments illustrating children's storybooks, since finding full time work as an illustrator was difficult to impossible. She was seriously thinking about taking a job as a typist when a Philadelphia greeting card company offered her a position on their staff. This company specialized in steel engraving line cuts. There she began learning more about the commercial end of the illustrating business.

From Philadelphia, she moved to New York with portfolio in hand and one day she sought shelter from the rain in a greeting card store. She admired their greeting card line, made note of the publishers' name and called for an appointment for a job interview. She was hired by the firm of Ars Sacra, which later became Crestwick, Inc. Her work was to design illustrations for cards, books,and advertising posters, all dealing with juvenile subjects, that were to be produced in full color. She was a very happy lady!

It was here that she created her now famous characters - the impish "Shabby O'Hair," his little sister "Raggy Muffin," Shabby's plump mother "M'Lady O'Hair," his father "Sinclair N. O'Hair," the inimitable little dog "Waggy," Shabby's good friend "Stuffy Duffy," and other delightful creations which have warmed the hearts of everyone who sees them. A close relative tells me "Charlot's work depicted her to a 'T.' She could be cheerful, bouncy, and full of life, like her Redheads, and also quite, serene, and religious like her other figurines. If you look closely you may see a touch of her personality in every sketch, card, and figurine that she designed."

She incorporated her pets into her artwork and the figurines. You will find Mia, the cat, Hansy, the dachshund, and Fritzy, the Schnauzer with many of her figurines.

Franz Goebel, the fourth generation head of W. Goebel Porzellanfabrik, noticed her artwork on the greeting card line and she was soon invited to visit the production facility. Her employment with W. Goebel brought her art form from the flat sheet of paper into the three-dimensional. Here her characters took life-like form with all the mischief and impish qualities we all admire so much today. Her first figurine, "Strike," was modeled by the master sculptor Arthur Moeller and the mold date on the bottom of that figurine is 1957. The factory records indicate that the work was assigned for sculpting November 16, 1956. More than 100 different figurines were designed, molded, and produced before the series ultimately ceased in 1988. Gerhard Skrobek worked with her on 64 different figurines and together they made a great team, though not without some "artist disagreements" as you might suspect. "Charlot was a perfectionist. She would not agree to a change simply for cost sake." Each had their own idea of how the drawing should be transformed into a three-dimensional form, but together they produced a wonderful series. She was under exclusive contract to Goebel until 1980, when illness forced her to cut back on her designing.

Working with Miss Byj, Goebel master sculptors Arthur Moeller and Gerhard Skrobek fashioned the initial four Redhead figurines "Strike," "The Roving Eye," "Oops," and "Little Miss Coy."

Her artwork features children and motherhood in two distinctive styles. One style was the very popular "Redheads" as the Goebel Charlot Byj Redheads became known, and the other style was the blonde series of approximately 16 different figurines. The redheaded children are always bouncy characters, full of life and mischief, but fully charming. The blondes are more serene and gentle in their young approach to life. There were a few figurines that were also painted as children with brown hair.

Charlot's charming little characters were produced by the Goebel Company from 1957 until 1988 in a variety of forms. Certainly, the most popular were the figurines but they also appeared as annual baby ornaments, annual

Christmas ornaments, an annual plate series, art prints, and three different music boxes which utilized the figurines as the center pieces. There were also three different lamps, only one of which was placed in Goebel production. Last, but not least in importance, they produced the dolls in a variety of different sizes. The doll series production continues today with Goebel doll designer Karen Kennedy translating the original artwork of Charlot Byj into Goebel dolls.

The appeal and success were immediate, for these lovable youngsters tugged at everyone's heart. The result was the more than 100 items that were produced by Goebel and are eagerly sought after by active collectors today. Their appeal is as timeless today as when first introduced.

Charlot loved living in New York City. She loved the theater and the operas, and attended almost all of the exhibits that came to the Metropolitan Museum, since she lived only two blocks away. Although her free time was limited, she loved to travel and was an avid reader. She loved skiing and going to the shore, as she enjoyed both the mountains and the ocean. Holidays always found her at home with relatives and friends. Charlot was a caring and sincere person, and that is exemplified in all her works. Her nature is encapsulated in the following recollection by Joan N. Ostroff, entitled "In Memoriam."

"Charlot Byj"

Mischievous. Impish. Witty. Redhead.
Gentle. Tender. Precious. Blonde.
Charlot Byj

A woman of unlimited insight into the cherished innocence of childhood, Charlot was forever setting down on paper her inner visions of this all-too-brief time of life. Her drawings seemed to appear as if magic, just in one steady flow from her heart to paper.

Those fortunate enough to have known her personally delighted in witnessing all the aspects of this remarkable talent. Those who know her through her figurines, faithful translations into three dimensions by Goebel of West Germany of both the Redhead and the Blonde series, are not disappointed, for Charlot's spirit shines through.

Charlot the person is deeply missed. Charlot Byj the artist is still with us. For that we can give thanks.

The world lost a very talented artist on August 7, 1983.

HISTORY OF W. GOEBEL

Over a century ago, January 31, 1871, at the foot of the fabled Coburg Castle in Oeslau, Germany, Franz Detleff Goebel and his son, William, founded F. & W. Goebel Company as manufacturers of marbles, slates, and slate pencils known as Thuringian ware. It was not until eight years later that the Duke of Saxon of Coburg granted permission for a kiln for porcelain-making to be built on the factory grounds. Franz and William were great innovators of their time, as has each of their descendants up to the present generation who guide this internationally recognized industry.

To be sensitive to the present, devoted to the past, and open to the future, are the rare qualities that characterize a farsighted, progressive entrepreneur. It is this combination that has enabled W. Goebel to grown harmoniously and progressively from its early development to its status today.

Never satisfied that what they were producing, these creative men expanded their production to be of greater use to more people. They developed a line of utilitarian and handsome porcelain coffee services, milk pitchers and eggcups - all manner of objects to make eating a pleasant entertainment.

Just as 1900 brought forth a new era and a new century, F. & W. Goebel Company made their contribution to progress by introducing porcelain figurines in 1911, and these figurines launched the company on the way to international fame. The area of Bavarian where they were situated, and Rodental, where the present W. Goebel factory is located, have been noted for a particularly high standard of craftsmanship and artistic skill for generations. It is this appreciation of the genuine among its artists that has so contributed to the inherent quality of the House of Goebel products.

When Franz Detleff Goebel died in 1909, his son, William expanded the already flourishing enterprise by realizing the wisdom of exporting their products abroad. It was he who opened up the demand for W. Goebel products on an international scale.

Max Louis Goebel succeeded his father, William, in 1911, and his enormous contribution to the expansion of the firm was twofold. He not only had a tremendous creative flair, but he knew how to take the fullest advantage of his very sophisticated technical equipment. He expanded the markets at home and abroad with a widely diversified group of objects d'art and attractive pieces for the home.

1929 ushered in a new generation. Franz Goebel, in close cooperation with his mother, Frida, and his brother-in-law, Dr. Eugen Stocke, began a three-decade direction of the firm. There were great strides made in constantly advancing technical improvements and expansion of production facilities.

1935 was one of the most auspicious years in the entire history of the Goebel family. It marked the year that the first collection of "M. I. Hummel" figurines appeared. These three-dimensional adaptations of Sister Marie Innocentia Hummel's enchanting sketches of the recollection of her childhood have captured the heart of collectors all over the world. W. Goebel has exclusive worldwide production and distribution rights for all "M. I. Hummel" figurines.

Arthur Moeller and Reinhold Ungar modeled the first "M.I. Hummel" figurines right in the Goebel studios under the personal and concerned supervision of Sister M. I. Hummel, and each year their names become more and more important to the collectors of her exquisite work.

They have been joined in the Goebel studios in succeeding years by such illustrious names as Walt Disney; Hans Schaubach; Kathe Kruse; Maria Spotl; Lore; Charlot Byj; Hanns Welling and Michel Thomas. Among the W. Goebel artists, Gerhard Bochmann and Gerhard Skrobek, creators of the rare and magnificently wrought "Wild Life" series, are internationally recognized as two of the finest innovative sculptors of our day.

Toys joined the family of W. Goebel products in 1950, and, in 1967, they were put into expanded production in a new, totally modern toy factory. That same year, W. Goebel founded Oeslauer Manufaktur which has been developing porcelain dinner ware with ceramic glazes, a very innovative entry into the dinnerware field. The unexpected and premature death of Franz Goebel ended an active and creative life. He left not only a legacy of being loved by all, but an immensely successful corporate entity consisting of subsidiaries both in Germany and abroad.

In 1969, Wilhelm Goebel and Ulrich Stocke, became the fifth generation of this unique manufacturing family, to lead the Goebel group in the creative tradition of their ancestors and with a constantly expanding view of the future and its needs.

Since 1971, Goebel has added a number of new groups manufacturing a variety of products with entirely new concepts. W. Goebel & Co., Meudt, produces a stunning collection of lamps. Merkelbach Manufaktur, Hohr-Grenzhausen, manufactures salt-glazed leadless stoneware. Strikingly handsome, they are hand-engraved in designs that have been traditional for generations. Exciting glass, drinking ware and accessories are being produced by Charlottenhutte, Werdohl. The latest member of the Goebel enterprise is Cortendorf Vertrieb, Coburg, whose faiences, ceramics and art objects are further indicators of the diversity of Goebel's management thinking and its ambition to create the best of everything to meet the demands of their customers and the collectors around the world.

During this period of time, a number of trademarks have been used. The Crown mark, the full bee, the modified bee, the three line, Goebel with the modified bee and finally the trade mark used today. There are many variations and combinations of these various marks as illustrated below.

For the purpose of studying those figurines designed by Charlot Byj, only trademarks (TMK) 3, 4, 5, and 6 are applicable

Mark		First Used
1	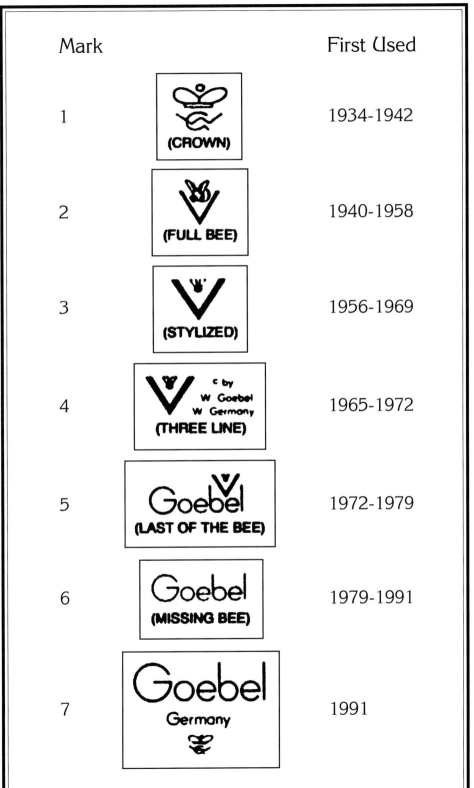 (CROWN)	1934-1942
2	(FULL BEE)	1940-1958
3	(STYLIZED)	1956-1969
4	c by W Goebel W Germany (THREE LINE)	1965-1972
5	Goebel (LAST OF THE BEE)	1972-1979
6	Goebel (MISSING BEE)	1979-1991
7	Goebel Germany	1991

11

INTRODUCTION TO THE SCULPTORS

Gerhard Bochmann

Dresden, an artists dream, was the birthplace, on November 16, 1925, of Gerhard Bochmann. With an imagination enriched by the surroundings containing art work dating back to the Baroque period, justifying Dresden's name as a second Florence, it is no wonder that young Gerhard's thoughts turned to sculpting.

Even before entering school, he began working with clay. As his interests and artistry developed he left school with his parent's permission to become an apprentice at the famed Meissen Porcelain Company. He accomplished the difficult entrance examination in 1940 and was privileged to work under the direction of the artist, Willy Jahnig.

With Meissen, his real apprenticeship began under the instructors E. Oehme and Professor Erich Hosel, both of whom had studied fine arts under Ernst Barlach. Following the war, Bochmann returned to Meissen and began remodeling the treasured ancient Meissen figurine works by renowned Kaendler.

In 1962, he became an employee of W. Goebel, where he soon became one of only two master sculptors. His talents contributed to a broad variety of items, including the limited edition, (which is now closed), of the "Pioneer Perennial" collection, the elegant "Wildlife" collection and the "Eden Gallery." He is the creator of "Fashions On Parade" and translated the charming designs of Lore into "Blumenkinder" figurines.

Bochmann retired from Goebel September 1, 1991.

Figurines Sculpted by Bochmann:

Byj 43: Just Hitched (Wall plaque)

Byj 44: Lucky Day	Byj 61: First Degree
Byj 45: Dropping In	Byj 62: Swinger
Byj 46: The Way To Pray	Byj 63: Nurse
Byj 48: Copper Topper	Byj 72: Damper On The Camper
Byj 49: Trim Lass	Byj 73: Heads Or Tails
Byj 50: Cheer Up	Byj 74: Wash Day
Byj 51: Let It Rain	Byj 75: Sea Breeze
Byj 52: Skater's Waltz	
Byj 53: Little Shopper	

Theo Menzenbach

Theo Menzenbach was born August 21, 1930. He joined Goebel October 1, 1948, and left Goebel December 31, 1961.

Figurines sculpted by Menzenbach:

Byj 15: Starling plaque	Byj 22: Off Key
Byj 16: Bless Us All	Byj 23: The Kibitzer
Byj 17: A Child's Prayer	Byj 26: Good News

Arthur Moeller

Arthur Moeller was born January 1, 1886, in Rudolstadt/Thuringen, Germany. His first schooling began in 1900 at the studio for ceramics in Rudolstadt, followed by working in several different Thuringian porcelain factories. Studies continued at the Academy of Art in Dresden and at the Academy of Art Munich, as a student of Professor Wadere. Following his participation as an exhibitor with Munich Art in 1910 at the Petit Plais in Paris he was hired by Max Louis Goebel on July 1, 1911 where his main job was to "invent little plastic articles."

He was a regular participant at exhibitions of art in Munich, Prague, Bayreuth, Kulmbach and Coburg. In 1934, Franz Goebel entrusted Moeller and Reinhold Unger (another Goebel master sculptor) with the transformation of the two dimensional drawings of artist M. I. Hummel to three-dimensional figurines.

With Unger, he became the father of the German Disney characters in ceramic. He modeled the Disney figurines "Lady and the Tramp" and the children's plate series of "Davy Crockett."

Moeller spent nearly 50 years working at Goebel when he died in 1972 at age 86. He was a master in designing and sculpting articles of a diminutive form. This special ability enabled him to contribute a vast array of products to Goebel Porzellanfabrik

Figurines sculpted by Moeller:

Byj 1: Strike	Byj 7: Atta Boy
Byj 3 -Oops	Byj 11: Sleepy Head
Byj 5: Shear Nonsense	Byj 12: Sitting Pretty
Byj 6: A Young Man's Fancy	Byj 18: The Stolen Kiss

Naumann (First name unknown)

He was a free-lance sculptor and did only one Byj item.

Figurine sculpted by Naumann:

Byj 33: Upside down umbrella with candy cane as handle.

Gerhard Skrobek
Master sculptor - W. Goebel Porzellanfabrik

Gerhard Skrobek, a master sculptor of the Goebel Company, was born in Silesia, the northernmost part of Germany, subsequently moving with his family to Berlin. There, surrounded by museum art treasures and encouraged by his artist mother, young Skrobek became immersed in the heady climate of artistic tradition. From early childhood, he was fascinated with sculpture and its many artistic forms. He studied at the Reimannschule in Berlin, a renowned private academy of the arts. Later, he continued his studies in Cobourg. Through one of his professors, he was introduced to porcelain sculpture at W. Goebel Porzellanfabrik.

Skrobek joined Goebel in 1951 and soon became one of its leading sculptors and eventually the predominate interpreter of Sister Maria Innocentia Hummel's drawings into three-dimensional form.

It is obvious, when you examine the number of figurines that he sculpted from the artwork of Charlot Byj, that he was the most prolific sculptor to work with her. He created sixty figurines of the one hundred and ten Charlot Byj designs that were produced by Goebel. Together they made an excellent team!

According to his interpretation, Skrobek is able to capture the life and vitality of the two-dimensional art through the use of a textured surface in the sculpting process. Skrobek is articulate and personable, and a delight to meet and to talk with about M. I. Hummel figurines.

Figurines sculpted by Skrobek:

Byj 2: The Roving Eye
Byj 4: Little Miss Coy
Byj 8: O'Hair For President
Byj 9: E-e-eek
Byj 10: Springtime
Byj 24: Daisies Won't Tell
Byj 25: Putting On The Dog
Byj 36 -Mother Embracing Child
Byj 37: Rock-A-Bye-Baby
Byj 38: Evening Prayer
Byj 47: Byj Display Plaque
Byj 54: Little Prayers Are Best
Byj 55: Tender Shepherd
Byj 56: Her Shining Hour
Byj 57: Madonna Of The Doves
Byj 58M: Rock-A-Bye-Baby (music box)
Byj 59: Little Prayers Are Best
Byj 60M: Skater's Waltz (music box)
Byj 64: Love Bugs
Byj 64M: Love Bugs (music box)
Byj 65: Bongo Beat

Byj 66: Baby Sitter
Byj 67: Trouble Shooter
Byj 68: Say A-aa-aah
Byj 69: Bachelor Degree
Byj 76: Barbecue
Byj 77: 1-2 Ski Doo
Byj 78: Lazy Day
Byj 79: Camera Shy
Byj 80: Boy With Afghan Hound
Byj 81: Condiment set
Byj 82: Condiment set
Byj 83: Fore
Byj 84: Bird Watcher
Byj 85: Captive Audience
Byj 86: Once Upon A Time
Byj 87: Four Letter Word For Ouch
Byj 88: Something Tells Me
Byj 89: Yech
Byj 90: Nothing Beats A Pizza
Byj 91: A Funny Face From Outer Space

Byj 92: Dear Sirs
Byj 93: Yeah Team
Byj 94: Not Yet A Vet
Byj 95: Bedtime Boy
Byj 96: Bedtime Girl
Byj 97: All Gone
Byj 98: Sweet Snacks
Byj 99: Sharing Secrets
Byj 100: Farm Friends
Byj 101: Come Along

Byj 102: Please Wait
Byj 103: Staying Fit
Byj 104: Almost There
Byj 105: The Collector
Byj 106: The Practice
Byj 107: Shall We Dance
Byj 108: Greetings
Byj 109: A Special Friend
Byj110: Communion.

Karl Wagner

He was born March 30, 1900, in Holenbrunn/Oberfranken. At the age of 16, he entered the Nuremberg School of Arts where his work won one award and six commendations. From 1920 to 1922 he studied at the academy of Stuttgart, where he worked with Professor Habich. After completing his studies at the Academy, he entered the ceramics industry as an artist/sculptor, where he worked for 16 years. In 1936, he joined the W. Goebel Porzellan-fabrik as a sculptor.

In 1949, after 13 years with Goebel, he was given the responsibility as master sculptor for the new toy division of the company, Hummelwerk-Spielwaren KG. This new responsibility encompassed the modeling and technical preparations of all the products including the toy animals and the "M. I. Hummel" dolls. Before retiring in 1972, he created many figurines for Goebel including several for "M. I. Hummel" and Disney. Two years following his retirement, Wagner died on December 4, 1974.

Figurines sculpted by Wagner:
Byj 29:Calorie Counter
Byj 35: Spring Cleaning
Byj 41: Pretzel Lena.

Helmut Wehlt

Born May 7, 1915 he joined Goebel September 1, 1954, and left Goebel June 30, 1960.

Figurines sculpted by Wehlt:
Byj 21: Moon Light Sonata (wall plaque)
Byj 27: Plenty Of Nothing
Byj 28: Gangway
Byj 32: Standing Man & Woman (salt & pepper shakers).

Rudi Wittman

Born June 24, 1921, Wittman joined Goebel February 5, 1953, and retired from Goebel July 1, 1984.

Figurines sculpted by Wittman:
- Byj 70: Lamp - birchtree trunk with Byj 6 - A Young Man's Fancy (not produced - samples only)
- Byj 71: Lamp - birchtree trunk with Byj 10 - Springtime (not produced- samples only)

Ewald Wolf

Born April 29, 1912, he joined Goebel November 8, 1950, and left Goebel December 31, 1961. He died December 4, 1968.

Figurines sculpted by Wolf:
- Byj 19: Spellbound
- Byj 20: Forbidden Fruit
- Byj 30: Girl with muff and tray (salt & pepper shaker with tray)
- Byj 31: Gingerbread Boy & Girl with Sled (salt & pepper shaker with sled as tray).

HOW FIGURINES ARE MADE

As you pick up one of Charlot Byj's wonderful figurines and admire it, the question comes to mind "how come these little cuties cost so much? All they do is make a mold, pour in some stuff, then fire it and paint it, right?" Wrong! Turning a drawing into one of these wonderful collectible figurines takes many more steps than most of us realize. With a lot of help from the staff at W. Goebel Porzellanfabrik in Rodental, Germany, perhaps the following information will help you understand the tedious and time consuming process of creating a figurine.

The process begins when a Goebel Master Sculptor studies a piece of original artwork – a drawing or painting by an artist, in our case, Charlot Byj. Because the artwork is only two dimensional, the sculptor must be able to envision the unseen details and execute them in a style that is consistent with the artist's concept. The painting may have included elements that are impossible to reproduce in a figurine, such as a flying bird. The sculptor must determine whether to include or exclude that detail or even modify it slightly, perhaps by merely placing the bird on the shoulder of the main figurine.

Sculpting may take several weeks until a suitable model is completed in plasteline. A combination of one-half beeswax and one half clay, plasteline gives the Master Sculptor complete control. As an example, if an artist sculpts a figurine with arms upward and a week later decides to lower them, it can accomplished merely by repositioning them; the artist's own body temperature will soften the beeswax within the clay.

Next, a model-maker cuts the figurine into parts to be reproduced in a series of individual molds. Complicated figurines may require more than 30 single molds. The mold-maker then prepares a separate "mother" mold for each individual part.

In order not to confuse you with a variety of mold names, please understand that a total of three types of *molds* and *models* must be made – a set of "mother" *molds*, a set of "working" *models* and a set of "working" *molds*.

The mold-maker uses each of the individual parts of the clay model from which to make the "mother" *molds*. These clay parts are so soft and fragile that they can only be used once. Therefore, a set of "working" *models* (in a positive image) is made from the "mother" *molds*. The "working" *models* may be cast in acrylic resin which is as hard as steel and thereby assures a standard or non-growing size variation of figurines produced by a series of "working" *molds*. These "working" *models* are used to make a set of "working" *molds*. It is the plaster of Paris "working" *mold* which is used to cast the figurine. Each "working" *mold* can produce approximately 20 castings before the mold looses it sharp detailing and must be replaced to assure the high quality standards imposed by Goebel.

So far it is not as easy as you originally imagined, correct? Please read on.

Now we begin the casting of the figurine. Every part, as determined by the model-fitter, must be cast separately. Liquid ceramic known as "slip" is poured into the plaster working molds. The plaster of the mold absorbs the moisture from the slip. As the slip thickens, it creates a thin hollow shell of ceramic. After the excess slip is pour out, the moist shell is removed for assembly into a complete figurine.

Each separate figurine shell and its parts must be assembled by hand, using thickened liquid slip to hold the parts together. Usually one assembler completes individual figurines as opposed to an assembly line process. Once these parts are assembled into a figurine, they are dried at room temperature. Until fully assembled, all parts must be kept at the same humidity so the completed figurine will dry and bake at a consistent rate. Before firing, a small hole is placed in the figurine in an inconspicuous place. Without the hole, the air inside the figurine would expand during the firing process causing the figurine to explode.

Once completed and dried, the figurines are fired at an intense temperature, three times during the production process.

The first firing at 2100 degrees Fahrenheit bakes the figurine into its white *bisque* stage. The piece is then coated with a glaze, using a spray gun and a powder-blue bath of liquid glaze. After a second firing at 1870 degrees Fahrenheit, the figurine is a glossy white (as the glaze has been melted into a thin glassy skin coating the entire surface) and is called "whiteware." After painting, the figurine will be fired a third time to permanently bond the color to the figurine.

The paints used on each Charlot Byj figurine were carefully selected especially to match the colors employed in her artwork. Master painters prepared samples to guide the highly trained painters who decorate the actual figurines. Since the figurines were painted by hand each piece is unique. Exceptional skill and quality control assure that each figurine made in the later years of production looks exactly like the same product made in the earlier years of production.

The faces are the most difficult part of the figurines to paint, and it is the artist who paints the face that places his or her initials on the bottom of each figurine. Some of the painting is so fine that the details are painted with brushes containing only one or two hairs.

It is interesting to note that the figurines designed by Charlot Byj are painted on top of the glaze. This accounts for the dull finished appearance of each figurine. If glazed after the painting, the result would be a very shiny surface over the paint. You may occasionally encounter a figurine that was glazed after the painting was completed – but this will usually be found only on the trademark 3 figurines.

Once the decorating or painting of each figurine is completed, it undergoes the "décor" firing at 1100 degrees Fahrenheit that permanently bonds the paints to each figurine, bringing it to life.

The skills required to successfully complete a figurine, as you can see, are quite high. These skills do not come inexpensively. To assure the company of adequate artists, Goebel offers five different Apprentice Programs: sculpting, mold-making, casting and assembly, painting and business administration.

Applicants for sculpting and painting must submit a portfolio of paintings, drawings and sculpture. They must also pass a series of tests taken over a three-day period. Very few applicants are accepted into the Sculpting Apprentice Program. Once accepted into the program, they must successfully complete a three-year apprentice program. The program is comprised of studies in drawing, painting, sculpture, design and technical training in porcelain making in the Bavarian State School for Porcelain in Selb, Germany.

In the first year of the apprentice program, the apprentice mainly watches and imitates a master painter and master sculptor at work. The second year, the apprentice spends fifty percent of the time designing. In the third year, apprentices can be more creative, and may spend a lot of time creating on their own.

CHARLOT BYJ FIGURINES AS COLLECTIBLES: CONDITIONS, VARIATIONS, AND VALUES

Are all figurines collectible?

There are 110 numbers in the series of Charlot Byj items with a doubling of number 64 for the figurine and the music box, which makes 111 pieces.

Of these, 8 numbers were produced in sample form only and not made for production and/or distribution:

Byj 12: open number,
Byj 13: open number,
Byj 70: Lamp with birch tree trunk incorporating Byj 6: Young Man's Fancy
Byj 71: Lamp with birch tree trunk incorporating Byj 10: Springtime
Byj 80: Boy with Afghan Hound
Byj 81: condiment set
Byj 82: condiment set
Byj 110: Communion.

Then, we have the 11 functional items:

Byj 15: Starling (wall plaque)
Byj 21: Moon Light Sonata (wall plaque)
Byj 29: Calorie Counter (wall plaque)
Byj 30: Girl, muff and tray (salt & pepper shaker)
Byj 31: Gingerbread boy and girl with sled (salt and pepper shaker with tray)
Byj 32: Standing man and woman (salt and pepper shaker)
Byj 33: Upside down umbrella with candy cane handle (candy dish)
Byj 34: Old Man Street Cleaner with Cart (toothbrush and tooth-paste holder)
Byj 35: Spring Cleaning (pencil and note pad holder)
Byj 42: Lamp featuring canopy covered bed incorporating Byj 38 Evening Prayer figurine
Byj 43: Just Hitched (wall plaque featuring honeymoon couple on buckboard seat).

There are three music boxes:

Byj 58M: Rock-A-Bye Baby
Byj 60M: Skater's Waltz
Byj 64M: Love Bugs

Finally, Byj 41 Pretzel Lena is considered, by some, to be a functional item and is very difficult to locate. Byj 54, the first version of Little Prayers Are Best, is also very difficult to locate.

To recap then we have:

	111	Numbers in the series
Less	8	Items not made or prototype samples only - next to impossible
Less	11	Functional items - very difficult to find
Less	3	Music boxes - they are available!
Less	2	Difficult to locate figurines

This provides us with **87** collectible items plus the chase, which is half of the fun, for the other 16 items that were produced but are difficult to locate. Good hunting!

Condition

Condition is all-important in any collectible and this certainly applies to the figurines designed by Charlot Byj. Pristine condition is always the most desirable. However, with age, handling, cleaning, moving, and other perils, some of our collectibles may become damaged. Those inevitable chips, flakes and breaks unfortunately occur. Not only do they deter in the eye appeal of the figurines, they also adversely affect the value of a prized figurine. Usually, a chip or flake may reduce the value of an item by 25 percent or more, depending on the prominence and position of the damage. If on the face of the figurine, the value may be affected even more.

Should a damaged Byj figurine be ignored and not purchased because it has a flake or chip? I would suggest that it will depend on the scarcity of that particular item. I know of a collection that includes two specimens of Byj 41: Pretzel Lena. One example is perfect in every detail and would be shown proudly in any collection. The other example was obviously dropped at some point in its life and the head was broken off at the neck. Someone quickly glued it back together and did an extremely poor job of repair. Would I purchase the damaged item? Certainly! It is truly one of the most sought after pieces of the entire series. Even damaged, I would enjoy having it in my cabinet until a better example came my way. Would I pay full price for the damaged Pretzel Lena? No, but I might pay 50 to 75 percent of the regular price for that particular item because of its rarity. Would I do the same for, perhaps, a Byj 16 Bless Us All? Again, no. If damaged in the same way and to such a great extent, I would pass over the damaged common item. I know that another example of the common item will surely, one day, come my way in undamaged condition.

Crazing

Some collectors will seek out the older pieces with the stylized trademark, TMK 3, feeling that the older pieces may have greater value. These pieces may also have a greater potential of crazing due to their age as well as the manner in which they have been stored over the years. Trade marks 4, 5 and 6 would naturally be less susceptible to crazing as they are more recent pieces; however, any figurine may be subject to crazing. Carefully check any early figurine that you consider purchasing for crazing damage! Does crazing affect the value of the figurines?

Well known Dorothy Dous, president of "Hummel Collectors Club, Inc.," 1261 University Drive, Yardley, Pennsylvania 19067-2857, has published the Dorothy Dous Inc. Crazing Chart which may be used as a "guideline" to the reduction in value due to crazing of a figurine. I quote, with her permission, from her copyrighted chart as follows:

Area(s) Crazed	Light	Severe
Under base only	25%	30%
On base top only	35%	40%
Under & top of base only	45%	50%
Figurine only (not face)	50%	60%
Figurine only (including face)	60%	65%
All (not face)	70%	75%
All (including face)	75%	80%

She defines Light Crazing as "normal vision provides that the craze mark(s) are **undetectable** at a distance of 18." Severe Crazing is defined as " normal vision provides that the craze mark(s) are **detectable** at a distance of 18."

In other words, a figurine with light crazing under the base only, that has a value, if perfect, of $100.00 may be only worth $75.00. Yes, crazing does affect the value of your collectible figurine.

Her firm offers a service whereby crazing may successfully be removed from any figurine. If your collection includes a figurine that is badly crazed you may want to contact her.

Master Painter Samples

If you have had the opportunity to visit the Goebel Porzellanfabrik in Rodental, Germany you probably also took the factory tour. During the tour you were able to observe the slip being poured into the molds, saw the slip hardened sufficiently to be removed from the molds, then watched with fascination as the artists began the tedious job of assembling all the various parts to make a complete figurine. Once the figurine was assembled, it then went to the ovens where it was turned into bisque, which is the fired but unglazed and unpainted figurine.

After being fired to the bisque stage, the figurines are dipped into a glazing solution and fired once again. At this point, they go to the painters who complete the process of making these little bits of clay into the treasures we enjoy today.

It is here that we become aware of the Master Painter Samples. Sitting atop each painter's stand is a figurine which the painter uses as the guide to complete the painting of the series of figurines that he or she is painting at that time. Currently, there is a metal tag attached to the specimen that is being used as a model. That tag reads "Meister Maler." This tag is attached by a small plastic band. In years gone by, the master painter samples usually had a fine red line painted around the entire base of the figurine. This was the manner in which painters were assured of meeting the specifications of the master painter.

The artist that paints the face and facial features places their initials on the base of the figurine. That same painter may or may not complete the painting of that figurine. More than likely, the figurine is passed on to another painter who will do some or all of the remaining painting.

I am told by one of the former master painters that it was typical that there would be 20 to 25 master painter samples for each figurine design that was produced. Sometimes they were broken or lost, and they did need samples for all the painters to use.

Are they collectable? You bet they are! Most serious collectors would like very much to have a master painter sample in their collection. Me included!

W. Goebel Porzellanfabrik Archives Collection.

Color Variations

Color variations are very interesting to the serious collector of Charlot Byj figurines. Each figurine has been accurately described based on examination of examples from our own collection, private collections or information in the factory records, which include factory production records and the colored brochures or catalogue pages illustrating one or more figurines. There are evidences of, shall we say, "artistic license," where the painting does not conform to the "normal" standards. This may be something as simple as the shirt on the boy, which may regularly be painted as a black and white check, being left unpainted and thereby appearing white or a dog's sweater being changed from black and white checks to a solid color. Unfinished? A mistake? A color variation? Perhaps, after the figurine was introduced, the factory decided that the color should be changed to "improve the sales appeal."

So, which came first - the chicken or the egg? In reality, what are described as variations are really the original paintings. The true variations are those varying from the original painting concepts. Please keep this fact in mind as you continue to read the descriptions.

More than likely, I believe, after examining many "color variations" that there was a simple matter of economics involved. Most of the real color variations that have been examined or reported have been from trademark 3, and perhaps a few from trademark 4. It would appear to me that the initial production of the figurines was very detailed in their painting. As the series became more popular and sales showed a significant increase, perhaps the factory decided there was a need to paint the figurines more simply in order to meet the increased production needs and reduce the production costs at the same time.

The most prominent examples of other color variations are having the normally painted redheaded child appear as a blonde or brunette. Or, as in the case of Byj 12, Sitting Pretty, the normally painted blonde girl being painted with red hair. There are many examples of color variations, and those of which I am aware I have listed following the description of each figurine. If your collection includes examples that are not listed, I would like very much to hear from you with a full description and a color photograph for my files. My address, telephone number and e-mail address is in the front of this book. Please contact me!

Again, a question will arise as to added value of a color variant. Any departure from the norm usually will add value to a collectible. This is the case with the Byj series of figurines, as the variant should have a slight increase in value. Most collectors who have color variants will have the regular painted piece displayed with the color variant(s) of that same piece in their cabinets. Add an unpainted piece of the same figurine(s) for even more interest!

As a Charlot Byj collector, you should know that in 1965 Goebel changed to lead free paints so the red used for hair and other items on the figurines may, from time to time, appear to be slightly lighter or different in color.

White or Unpainted Figurines

White or unpainted figurines appear on the market from time to time. These figurines actually have a white overglaze on their surface, which is done to prepare the surface for decorating. They are dipped in a light blue coating which, when fired, turns white. The question arises, "Are the whites really rare and more valuable pieces that I may want to collect?" Whether you want to collect them or not is a matter of personal preference, but they do add interest to a collection of Charlot Byj figurines. The stark contrast of the white figurine with the fully painted one is interesting. Your choice!

Now, are they rare? A correspondent friend of mine who lived in Germany at the time provided me with the following story. She said that while attending a "signing" of Goebel items at one of the Goebel dealer's stores, located in Germany, she met Christian Goebel, who, when asked about the white figurines replied, "the factory does not sell them, but, the employees do." They are sometimes referred to as "lunch box specials" by other dealers, which in a roundabout manner, confirms Mr. Christian Goebel's comment.

One further comment regarding the "overglazed whites": when the factory discontinued an item, there were occasions when the remaining inventory of unpainted items was boxed up and disposed of by selling them across the street at the factory store. They were subsequently sold to anyone wanting such a figure for their collection.

My personal preference is to have one or more of the interesting white unpainted figurines in a collection. Generally, when I have encountered them they were priced less than the regular price of a painted item. They are sought after and are collectible, either as a single "example" piece or, for a real challenge of collecting, as the entire series in the white unpainted format.

Determining the Value of Your Collection

We all want to know - "how much is it worth?" That is natural human curiosity, right? While all of the "Redhead" and "Blonde" figurines were produced by W. Goebel Porzellanfabrik, Germany, the Goebel Company does not "make" a secondary market for these items. The secondary market is influenced by a number of factors, most of which have been outlined above. Condition, rarity, color, eye appeal, and authenticity are some of the considerations that determine the value in the secondary market.

The Goebel Company does , however, provide a service to members of the M. I. Hummel Club who wish to buy or sell any Goebel collectible through their Collector's Market.

The Collector's Market computerizes buy and sell requests each month. If there is a match between a seller's desire to sell a specific figurine and a buyer's desire to purchase the same figurine, Goebel sends a list of persons for the buyer to contact. The buyer must complete the transaction with the seller, and Goebel takes no commission. This is a very nice service provided to M. I. Hummel Club Members, and, at no commission charges. If you are not presently a member of the M. I. Hummel Club, you may wish to contact them at the following address:

> M. I. Hummel Club
> Goebel Plaza
> P. O. Box 11, route 31
> Pennington, N. J. 08534-0011

There are several other methods you may consider if you decide to dispose of your collection. There are excellent newspapers that specialize in advertising antiques and collectibles. One is The Antique Trader, PO Box 1050, Dubuque, IA 52004-1050, 1-800-334-7165. The Antique Trader is a weekly publication that regularly has approximately 100 pages of advertisements covering a wide variety of antiques.

Another method is to join an association of Goebel collectors. One of the most prominent groups is The Goebel Networkers, PO Box 355, Hamburg, PA, 19526. The Goebel Networkers publishes a quarterly newsletter of approximately 16 pages focusing on many different figurines and related products manufactured by W. Goebel Porzellanfabrik.

If you plan to sell your collection, timing will also very definitely affect the value. Selling in a strong economic market will help assure higher prices. If you sell to an antique dealer, they must invest their capital, store the merchandise, advertise it, pack and ship it as well as, hopefully for them, make a profit. If you, therefore, sell to an antique dealer, you will receive less for your collection than if you are prepared to handle each of these transactions yourself.

Perhaps you want an appraisal of your collection for insurance purposes. You may find the name of a reputable appraiser in your local telephone directory or you may wish to call the American Society of Appraisers at 1-800-272-8258.

FIGURINE DESCRIPTION AND PRICING

The following listing and description is designed to enable the beginning and advanced collector to accurately determine which piece(s) you have in your collection and if you have an unusual color variation piece. There are occasions where a figurine is known by more than one name. Where this has occurred, the second name appears in parenthesis.

The pricing guide following each figure description is merely a guide. In the real market place, prices are determined by the price a buyer is willing to pay and for which a seller is willing to sell a figurine. I have been a student of Charlot Byj figurines for a number of years and have observed and recorded prices for which the figurines have sold over a period of time. These observations, coupled with my knowledge of which figurines are truly scarce, have been used in suggesting the retail price ranges. I have not created low prices in order to buy the scarce pieces for our own collection nor have I created artificially high prices in order to sell our collection. My attempt is one to be fair to both collectors and dealers. I might add that I have paid more for some figurines than the price range suggests and, certainly, I have also paid less.

My advice to you is if you truly want the figurine that you have just discovered and the price is reasonable buy it when you see it. It may be a long time until you have another opportunity to purchase the same figurine.

These prices are for regular painting, not the variations. Trademark 3 figurines usually command a higher value of 15 to 25 percent.

Byj 1. **Strike**: 4". Boy with red hair, wearing black and white checked shirt, green overalls which have a red patch with one dot on seat and red handkerchief with white dots in back left pocket, brown shoes. Black bowling ball on wooden floor. White base, top painted as wood. Color Variations: Known with red figure "8" painted on the bowling ball. Sculpted by Arthur Moeller. The original issue price was $6.00 in 1957. Price range: $70-95

Byj 2. **The Roving Eye**: 4 1/2". Boy with red hair, wearing black and white checked shirt, green overalls, red patch with white dots on right knee, reddish dog peering from behind boy's left leg. Boy has right eye open, left eye winking, hands held behind back. Dog wearing black and white checked sweater. Sculpted by Gerhard Skrobek. Color Variations: None known. The original issue price was $6.00 in 1957. Price range: $70-95

Byj 3. **Oops:** 4 3/4". Girl with red hair, green bow in hair, wearing plaid dress in two shades of green, white bow tied in back and red polka dots on white scarf on neck, black and white shoes with red bows. Black mother cat and two black kittens all with white paws walking in front of girl. All standing on white base, top painted as green grass. Sculpted by Arthur Moeller. Color Variations: Known with a green four leaf clover painted on the bottom of girls white underpants. The original issue price was $6.00 in 1957. Price range: $120-150

Byj 4. **Little Miss Coy:** 4 1/2". Girl with red hair, two green bows in hair, wearing yellow straw hat with black ribbon, white blouse, green and white checked skirt and red scarf with white polka dots by right arm. White underpants, black hose, black and white shoes with red bows on sides with one black button on each shoe. Standing on white base, top painted as green grass. Sculpted by Gerhard Skrobek. Color Variations: None known. The original issue price was $6.00 in 1957. Price range: $60-75

Byj 5. **Shear Nonsense** (Make It Short): 5". Boy with red hair, wearing black and white checked shirt, green overalls, black comb behind right ear, red mirror in right front pocket, standing on tan box, with scissors in right hand cutting hair of girl with red hair, she is sitting in chair with white drape covering her, drape has red and white patch over girl's left knee. Her black shoes resting on red foot stool. White base, top painted tan as wood. Red hair snips on tan floor . Sculpted by Arthur Moeller. Color Variations: Known with boy's hair painted blonde. The original issue price was $10.00 in 1957. Price range: $120-150

Byj 6. **A Young Man's Fancy:** 4 1/2". Girl with red hair, one green bow in hair, wearing orange dress with yellow polka dots, black hose, black and white shoes with red bow on side. Girl sitting on brown bench, looking down reading red painted book. Brown squirrel sitting on left top end of bench. Boy with red hair, wearing black and white checked shirt, green overalls and brown shoes, holding bunch of yellow flowers in left hand, approaching her from the right rear corner. Right hand on bench. Has green and yellow grass/flowers painted on white base. Sculpted by Arthur Moeller. Color Variations: Known with boy's hair painted blonde. The original issue price was $10.00 in 1957. Price range: $120-150

Byj 7. **Atta Boy** (Howdy): 4". Boy with red hair, wearing black and white checked shirt, green overalls, red patch with white dot on seat of overalls, black buttons on rear overall straps, brown shoes, hands raised to the front sides encouraging reddish dog with reddish/yellow sweater, standing on white base, top painted with green sprigs of grass and yellow flowers. Sculpted by Arthur Moeller. Color Variations: Known as above but with boy's hair painted blonde. Also known with dog's sweater painted black and white checks. Also known with dog's sweater painted mustard color and boy's overalls with green straps, white buttons with red cross in center and red patch with three dots on seat of overalls. The original issue price was $6.50 in 1957. Price range: $85-115

33

Byj 8. **O'Hair For President** (Lend Me Your Ears): 5 1/4". Boy with red hair, wearing black and white checked shirt, green overalls with red patch with white dot on seat of overalls, brown shoes, standing on tan/gray soap box with hands spread apart and in the air. Sculpted by Gerhard Skrobek. Color Variations: Known with painted solid black and gray over white to form the checked shirt, red patch on right knee with three white dots and white buttons with red crosses in center on back of green overall straps. The original issue price was $6.00 in 1957. Price range: $70-95

Byj 9. **E-e-eek:** 4 1/2". Girl with red hair, one green hair bow with white dots on bow, wearing green dress with white polka dots and white collar and trim on sleeves, black hose, black and white shoes with red bow, and black button on each shoe. Reddish dog wearing mustard colored sweater pulling down on girls white underpants. White base, top painted as green grass. Sculpted by Gerhard Skrobek. Color Variations: Known with girl's hair painted blonde, wearing green and white checked dress, black and white checked sweater on dog, no bow on shoes but two black painted buttons on shoes. The original issue price was $8.00 in 1957. Price range: $120-150

Byj 10. **Springtime** (Dreamhouse): 4 1/2". Boy with red hair, wearing black and white checked shirt, green overalls with red patch and two white dots on seat of overalls, brown shoes, holding hammer with tan handle in left arm and white bird house with red roof in right arm, walking to birch tree trunk which has two brown birds resting on top branch. Tree has green leaves, as does the white base, top painted as green grass. A heart and arrow is carved on the tree and there are two brownish flowers at the base of the tree. Sculpted by Gerhard Skrobek. Color Variations: Known with no patch on seat of overalls, but has red patch with three white dots on left knee, tree has brown trunk with two birds painted blue, green and black with white eyes resting on top branch. The birds are completely separated as they rest on the branch. Tree has green leaves sprouting and yellow and blue flowers at base. White base, top painted as green grass. TMK 3. The original issue price was $7.50 in 1957. Price range: $120-150

Byj 11. **Sleepy Head**: 5 1/2". Boy (yawning) with blonde hair dressed in blue pajamas with white polka dots, white rabbit house shoe on left foot, shoe off of right foot, holding gray/white teddy bear in left arm with right arm raised. Teddy bear has black eyes and nose and red mouth. Boy standing on white base, top painted pink. Sculpted by Arthur Moeller. Color Variations: As above but bear ears, front and rear paw soles and boy's house shoes are bright pink. TMK 3. The original issue price was $9.00 in 1957. Price range: $70-95

Byj 12. **Sitting Pretty:** 5". Girl with dark blonde hair, blue bow in hair, yellow straw hat that has a black ribbon on it behind head, dressed in blue dress with black bow at neck and white trim at edge of skirt and collar of dress, white petticoat, black shoes. Girl holding bouquet of flowers while sitting on gray round rock. Sculpted by Arthur Moeller. Color Variations: Known with girl's hair painted red, yellow straw hat has black edge and girl shyly looking down and to the right. The original issue price was $9.00 in 1957. Price range: $85-115

Byj 13. **Open number**

Byj 14. **Open number**

Byj 15. **Starling** (Wall plaque): Blonde hair boy in pink pajamas. Two white wings on his back. Right hand holding a metal star on a metal rod. Boy is lying facing right on a white cloud. The cloud has two yellow stars on the lower right front of the cloud. No base. Sculpted by Mensenbach. Color Variations: None known. The original issue price in 1957 is unknown. Price range: RARE

Byj 16. **Bless Us All:** 5 1/4". Boy with blonde hair, wearing light blue pajamas, hands folded in front on his chest, kneeling in prayer, on white base, top painted tan. Sculpted by Mensenbach. Color Variations: None known. The original issue price was $6.00 in 1957. Price range: $60-75

Byj 17. **A Child's Prayer:** 5 1/4". Girl with blonde hair, blue hair bow, wearing light blue nightgown with white polka dots and white trim at shoulders, sleeve cuffs, neck and across the back with bow tied in back, hands folded in front of her, kneeling in prayer on white base, top painted tan. Sculpted by Mensenbach. Color Variations: None known. The original issue price was $6.00 in 1957. Price range: $60-75

Byj 18. **The Stolen Kiss**: 5 1/2". Boy with red hair, wearing black and white checked shirt, green overalls with red patch - three white dots on right knee and red patch - 2 white dots on seat of overalls, black buttons on overall straps, brown sling shot in right rear pocket, brown shoes, hands on shoulders of blonde girl with blue hair bow, wearing blue dress with white trim at shoulders and collar and white bow in back, white petticoat and white shoes. Girl has painted flower bracelet on left wrist. Both standing on white base, top painted as green grass and white daisies with yellow centers. Sculpted by Arthur Moeller. Color Variations: Known as above but with two white dots on the patches of seat and knee of boy's overalls. The original issue price was $13.00 in 1957. Price range: $150-175

Byj 19. **Spellbound**: 5 1/2". Girl with red hair, green hair bow, wearing light green dress with white polka dots, white collar, trim at sleeves, petticoat and bow tied in back, black hose, black and white shoes with red bow on side and two black buttons on each shoe, sitting on brown book on school desk bench at school desk (desk and bench both have black legs), reading red book with "Spelling" on front cover alphabet A to E on inside page. Red apple sitting inside open book. Girl has green trim on eyes. All sitting on white base, top painted tan and stripes as wooden floor. Sculpted by Wolf. Color Variations: As above but with red pencil with black tip in hair, red trim on white collar, at sleeves and on petticoat. Alphabet A to Q inside book. TMK 3. Also known without green trim on eyes. The original issue price was $12.00 in 1958. Price range: $120-150

Byj 20. **Forbidden Fruit:** 4 1/4". Boy with red hair, wearing black and white checked shirt, green overalls with red apple in right and left rear pockets, brown shoes, walking on white base, top painted as green grass. Has several red apples in hands and has dropped three behind him. Sculpted by Wolf. Color Variations: None known. The original issue price was $7.00 in 1958. Price range: $120-150

Byj 21. **Moon Light Sonata (Moonshine Sonata) (**Wall Plaque): Boy with blonde hair, wearing black and white checked shirt, green overalls with red patch with white dot on seat of overalls, has left arm around girl with red hair, wearing green and white plaid dress, sitting on rooftop of building looking at blue sky with stars outlined in shape of heart, moon to the left. Laundry and building to their left and chimney to their right with crooked arrow coming out top. Sculpted by Wehlt. Color Variations: None known. The original issue price in 1958 is unknown. Price range: RARE

Byj 22. **Off Key:** 5 1/2". Boy with red hair, wearing black and white checked shirt, green overalls, brown shoes, strumming mustard colored banjo with left hand. He is reclining on red pillow in brown overstuffed chair with white doily on left and right arm and back of chair. Reddish dog looking from under right side of chair. Gray mouse, under chair cushion, peeping out of left side of chair. Green book - white pages under left rear corner of chair. Sculpted by Mensenbach. Color Variations: Also known with red line around face of banjo and white dots on the red pillow behind boy's head. The original issue price was $7.50 in 1958. Price range: $120-150

Byj 23. **The Kibitzer:** 4 3/4". Boy with red hair, wearing black and white checked shirt, green overalls with red patch and white dot on seat of overalls and black buttons on overall straps, brown shoes - hole in sole of right shoe, sitting on backward facing chair with right arm resting on chair back. Left arm raised and to the side. Reddish dog looking through back of chair. Color Variations: None known. The original issue price was $7.50 in 1958. Price range: $85-115

Right: Byj 24. **Daisies Won't Tell:** 4 1/4". Girl with red hair, two flower hair bows, wearing green dress with white polka dots, white collar and trim at sleeves and bow tied in back, red underpants, black hose, black and white shoes with red bows and one black button on each shoe. Girl holding single white flower in right hand and bouquet of flowers in left hand and arm, standing on white base. Tan sign lettered in red "Keep Off" stuck in green grass. Sculpted by Gerhard Skrobek. Color Variations: None known. The original issue price was $6.00 in 1956. Price range: $60-75

Byj 25. **Putting On The Dog:** 5". Girl with red hair, green hair bow, wearing green and white plaid dress, white petticoat, black hose and her mother's red high heeled shoes, holding handbag with red trim in left hand. Girl walking on white base, top painted as green grass, followed by two brown dachshunds with red bows on their collars, one dog with mustard colored sweater, the other dog with aqua sweater. Dog's noses up in the air. Sculpted by Gerhard Skrobek. Color Variations: Known with dog sweaters in green and white plaid to match girl's dress. TMK 3. The original issue price was $9.00 in 1956. Price range: $120-150

Byj 26. **Good News:** 4 1/2". Boy with red hair, wearing black and white checked shirt, green overalls, red patch with two white dots on right knee and red patch with three white dots on seat of overalls, white buttons with red cross on overall straps, brown shoes. Boy holding mustard colored bag marked in red "SOUR BALLS" in left hand and a bouquet of yellow flowers with green stems wrapped in white newspaper with "GOOD NEWS" as headlines in right hand. Standing on white base, top painted tan with green grass by right foot. Sculpted by Mensenbach. Color Variations: also known as above except: green overalls no patch on knee, no dots on patch on seat of overalls and with black buttons on overall straps The original issue price was $6.00 in 1958. Price range: $70-95

Byj 27. **Plenty Of Nothing:** 4 1/4". Boy with red hair, wearing black and white checked shirt, green overalls with red patch on right knee and black buttons on overall straps, brown shoes. Hands holding pockets inside out and a copper coin on ground between his shoes. Standing on white base, top painted as green grass. Sculpted by Wehlt. Color Variations: None known. The original issue price was $5.50 in 1958. Price range: $70-95

Byj 28. **Gangway;** 4 1/2". Boy with red hair, wearing black and white checked shirt, green overalls with red patch and white dot on seat with white envelope sticking out of right rear pocket, standing on a tan and brown striped "go-cart" with silver wheels. Green sign on left side of go-cart in white letters "P38." Reddish dog standing on back legs on go-cart, in front of boy, looking to the left. Bell/horn on front right side of go-cart. Sculpted by Wehlt. Color Variations: Known with dog looking straight ahead and bell on the front of cart. The original issue price was $8.50 in 1958. Price range: $120-150

Byj 29. **Calorie Counter** (Wall Plaque): 3 1/2" x 7". Heavy set red haired woman sitting on brown stool with red seat at soda fountain counter. She is wearing a green dress with white polka dots. Dress collar and sleeve cuff trimmed in red. Green hat with three daisies on brim and one red rose sticking up in the air from the brim of hat. Woman has bare feet with black and white shoes on the floor next to a white purse with a red clasp and green handle. Tan grocery bag with various vegetables showing at the top. She is using a straw to sip a pink soda with a red cherry on top. Counter top is black and soda dispenser is gray. Upper right corner of plaque has a yellow square with green lettering "The Calorie Counter." Sculpted by Karl Wagner. The original issue price in 1959 is unknown. Price range: RARE

Byj 30. **Girl bust salt shaker, Muff as pepper shaker and separate tray:** 3 1/2". Girl with long blonde hair pulled back and has red poinsettia in hair, white fur hat trimmed in black on head, wearing red cape trimmed with white fur and black accents. Cape has gold buttons on front. Girl wearing gold earrings. She is the salt shaker. In front of her is a white fur muff with black accents and a large red bow on top of muff. This is the pepper shaker. Both girl and muff resting on green free form tray. Sculpted by Wolf. The original issue price in 1959 is unknown. Price range: RARE

Byj 31. **Gingerbread boy and girl salt & pepper shakers with sled as tray:** 3" girl and 3 1/2" boy. Girl is pepper shaker with two holes on top and boy is salt shaker with 3 holes in top. Brown gingerbread man with black eyes and red mouth, nose and ears, gingerbread hat with white trim and green top, red, white and green collar at neck, gingerbread shoes with white, red, and green trim, green gloved left hand holding red and white candy cane. Brown gingerbread woman, hat decorated with white trim and red top, red bow at neck, white trim on coat, green mittens and white shoes. The sled is made of a pair of white with red stripe candy canes placed to resemble a sled. Sculpted by Wolf. The original issue price in 1959 is unknown. Price range: RARE

Byj 32. **Standing gingerbread man and woman salt & pepper shakers**: 3 1/2". woman and 3 3/4" man. Woman is salt shaker with three holes on top and man is pepper shaker with two holes on top. Gingerbread woman with white hat, trimmed with red and green bow, white trim at neck and muff on hands. Black eyes and mouth and red nose, three black buttons on front of coat. Black shoes with white trim. Gingerbread man with green flat top hat trimmed in white, black eyes and mouth and red nose and earmuffs. Green and white scarf at neck, three black buttons on front of coat, black shoes with white trim. Carrying red and white candy cane. Sculpted by Wehlt. The original issue price in 1959 is unknown.Price range: RARE

Byj 33. **Upside down umbrella candy dish:** 5" diameter. Candy dish shaped as upside down opened umbrella. Handle is white with green and gold stripes as a candy cane. Inside top of umbrella is red and the outside of umbrella is white. Edge trimmed in gold. Sculpted by Naumann. The original issue price in 1959 is unknown. Price range: RARE

Byj 34. **Old Man Street Cleaner:** 5 1/2". Old man with gray hair, eye brows and mustache, has blue hat with red brim on head, wearing white uniform with red patch with five white dots on seat of pants, four blue buttons on front of coat which has red stripe down left and right sleeves, blue shoes. Left arm is resting on red trash cart with white wheels trimmed in black. Right hand on cart. Sculpted by Karl Wagner. The original issue price in 1959 is unknown. Price range: RARE

Byj 35. **Spring Cleaning:** 5 1/2" tall and 5 1/4" wide. Woman with Broom holder for
pencil and note pad . Woman with red hair pulled up on top of head in "bun" wearing
light green skirt and dark green blouse with white polka dots. White apron with matching
green trim and large bow tied in back. Wearing red shoes. A white kitten with black eyes,
red nose and mouth sits in front of waste basket. The woman's broom handle is a pencil
and the basket behind her is for a note pad holder. Sculpted by Karl Wagner. The original
issue price in 1959 is unknown. Price range: RARE

Byj 36. **Mother Embracing Child:** 8 1/2".
Woman with blonde hair, pink wreath in hair,
holding blonde baby to her chest with both
arms. Mother and baby both dressed in white,
kneeling on white base with gold overlay.
Long stemmed roses on both left and right leg
coming up from the ground and small brown
rabbit close by mother's left knee. Sculpted by
Gerhard Skrobek. Color Variations: Also
known with brown overlay on base instead of
gold base.. The original issue price was $7.50
in 1959. Price range: $140-165

Byj 37. **Rock A Bye Baby:** 6 1/4".
Woman with long blonde hair, brown
hair ribbon, wearing long blue dress,
gold shoes, sitting on gray foot stool
which has gold legs with both arms
slightly raised, holding hands with a
small blonde baby dressed in white
gown. Baby sitting on woman's knee.
Sculpted by Gerhard Skrobek. Color
Variations: Also known with brown
shoes and brown legs on foot stool.
The original issue price was $8.00 in
1959. Price range: $85-115

Byj 38. **Evening Prayer:** 6 1/4". Girl with blonde hair, wearing light burgundy hair bow, blue nightgown with white trim at collar and edge of sleeves, with hands held in front of her, kneeling in prayer. Doll with blonde hair, wearing white nightgown with light burgundy polka dots, kneeling in prayer at her left knee. Girl and doll wearing light burgundy house shoes. No base on this figurine. Sculpted by Gerhard Skrobek. Color Variations: None known. The original issue price was $8.50 in 1959. Price range: $85-115

Byj 39. **Super Service:** 5 1/4". Boy with red hair, wearing black and white checked shirt, green overalls with red handkerchief in right rear pocket, brown shoes, wearing a white apron with bow tied in back, standing on mustard colored box. Boy holding telephone receiver in right hand and red pencil in left hand as he writes telephone order on white paper. Black telephone mounted on brownish wood, mustard colored basket filled with red apples in front of boy and nine cans stacked in front of apple basket. Sculpted by Arthur Moeller. Color Variations: None known. The original issue price was $9.00 in 1959. Price range: $150-175

Byj 40. **Guess Who:** 5". Girl with red hair, green hair bow, wearing white dress with greenish stripe , white underpants, black hose, black and white shoes with two black buttons on side. Girl has green eyes with black pupils. Boy with red hair, wearing black and white checked shirt, green overalls with black buttons on overall straps and red patch with two white dots on seat of overalls, brown shoes, his left hand behind his back and right hand is pulling girl's hair. Both standing on white base, top painted as green grass. Sculpted by Arthur Moeller. Color Variations: Known with boy's hair painted blonde. Also known without black buttons on overalls. The original issue price was $8.50 in 1958. Price range: $150-175

Byj 41. **Pretzel Lena:** 4 1/2". Girl with red hair in pigtails in circle on each side of head, wearing dark green dress with red, gold and green geometric design on front. Left arm holding long stick (pretzel holder - missing in photograph), kneeling with pink pig at right leg and tan pretzel tray in front of her. Sculpted by Karl Wagner. Color Variations: None known. The original issue price in 1958 is unknown. Price range: RARE

Byj 42. **Evening Prayer** (Lamp): Girl with blonde hair, wearing pink nightgown and blonde doll wearing blue nightgown (Byj 38), kneeling in prayer at edge of white covered canopy four poster bed. Bed has pink pillow and blue bed covering, both of which are trimmed in white. Gray kitten resting on bed next to pillow. Sculpted by Gerhard Skrobek. Color Variations: None known. The original issue price in 1958 is unknown. Price range: RARE

Byj 43. **Just Hitched** (Wall plaque): 4 1/2" by 4 3/4". Boy with red hair, wearing black and white checked shirt, green overalls, red handkerchief with white polka dots in left rear pocket, right hand holding left hand of girl with red hair, wearing yellow blouse and orange skirt or pants, holding decorated white hankie in her right hand. Both sitting on red board-type vehicle with black wheels and car crank. A man's brown shoe and a women's black shoe are tied to rear of vehicle. Plaque is white with green trim on upper edges and is in the shape of a heart Sculpted by Gerhard Bochmann. The original issue price in 1963 is unknown. Price range: RARE

Byj 44. **Lucky Day:** 3". Boy with red hair, wearing black and white checked shirt, green overalls and brown shoes, on his knees with right hand on green painted base and left hand nearly touching a green four leafed clover. Boy has green trim around eyes. Sculpted by Gerhard Bochmann. Color Variations: None known. The original issue price was $5.50 in 1963. Price range: $60-75

Byj 45. **Dropping In:** 5". Girl with red hair, two green hair bows, wearing light green blouse with green, white and black plaid jumper, pink hankie in right front pocket, white petticoat showing, black hose, black and white shoes, (no bows or black buttons), holding bouquet of gray/white flowers with red dot in center of flowers behind her back and standing on white base with reddish brown top. Sculpted by Gerhard Bochmann. Color Variations: None known. The original issue price was $6.00 in 1963. Price range: $70-95

Byj 46. **The Way To Pray:** 4 1/4". Girl with blonde hair, blue hair bow, wearing blue nightgown, positioning hands of small blonde boy wearing blue nightshirt. Both kneeling on white base with green painted top. Sculpted by Gerhard Bochmann. Color Variations: None known. The original issue price was $8.50 in 1963. Price range: $70-95

Byj 47. **Dealer Display Plaque:** 4 1/2". This plaque is a replica of the Byj 4, "Little Miss Coy," except, large white "sign board" to her left. Text painted on "sign board" varies and there are five known variations of this particular figurine. All figurines were sculpted by Gerhard Skrobek. The original issue price was $4.00 in 1966.

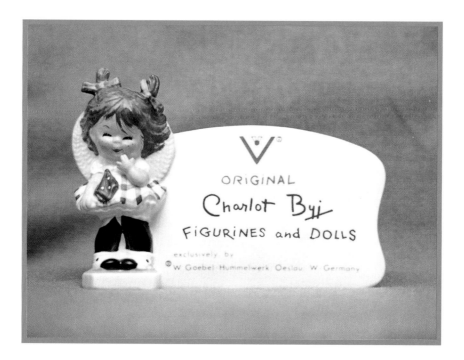

a. "TMK 3" followed by "Original" painted in blue followed by "Charlot Byj" followed by "Figurines and Dolls" painted in red followed by "exclusively by" followed by "W. Goebel-Hummelwerk. Oeslau W. Germany" painted in blue. TMK 4 on bottom of figurine. Price range: $150-175

b. "TMK 3" followed by "Original" printed in blue followed by "Charlot Byj" followed by "Redheads" followed by "Figurines and Dolls" printed in red followed by "exclusively by" followed by "W. Goebel, Rodental-Oeslau, W. Germany" printed in blue. TMK 4 on bottom of figurine. Price range: $150-175

c. "TMK 3" followed by "Original" painted in blue followed by "Charlot Byj" followed by "Redheads" followed by "Figurines" painted in red followed by "exclusively by" followed by "W. Goebel, Rodental, W. Germany" printed in blue.. TMK 4 on bottom of figurine. Price range: $100-125

d. "Original" - painted in blue followed by "Charlot Byj" followed by "Redheads" followed by "Figurines" painted in red followed by "exclusively by Goebel TMK 5" printed in blue. Price range: $100-125

e. "Original" painted in blue followed by "Charlot Byj" followed by "Redheads" followed by "figurines" painted in red followed by "exclusively by Goebel" followed by "W. Germany" painted in blue. TMK 6 on bottom of figurine. Price range: $100-125

Byj 48. **Copper Topper** (Forward March): 4 3/4". Girl with red hair, copper cooking pot on her head as hat, red tongue sticking out left side of her mouth, wearing yellow sweater, black and green plaid skirt, white stockings and black shoes - no bows or black buttons on shoes. Girl holding mustard colored spoon up in left hand as a baton and a red and white checked cloth in her right hand held at her waist. She is walking as though marching, on white base, top painted as green grass. Sculpted by Gerhard Bochmann. Color Variations: None known. The original issue price was $10.00 in 1967. Price range: $120-150

Byj 49. **Trim Lass:** 4 1/2". Girl with red hair, tan straw hat with red flowers and green leaves on head, wearing green, black and white checked blouse and white pants, red sandals. Girl pushing lawn mower with both hands, handle of mower painted red with black wheels, center of wheels green. All on white base, top painted as green grass. Sculpted by Gerhard Bochmann. Color Variations: None known. The original issue price was $14.00 in 1967. Price range: $120-150

Byj 50. **Cheer Up:** 5". Girl with red hair, wearing white nurse's cap, white nurse uniform including stockings and shoes, holding a golden basket with bow on top containing three red/yellow apples and a green leaf. Girl standing on white base, top painted as green tile. Sculpted by Gerhard Bochmann. Color Variations: None known. The original issue price was $8.00 in 1967. Price range: $85-115

Byj 51. **Let It Rain:** 6". Girl with red hair, wearing green dress and white pinafore, with red bug on her right front shoulder, black hose, black and white shoes with black bow and two black dots, her feet dangling in air. Girl's petticoat has black dot trim on edge. Boy with red hair, wearing black and white checked shirt, green overalls with red and white plaid patch with four black dots on left knee, black and white plaid patch on seat of overalls, and brown shoes. Both girl and boy sitting on red bench, holding a newspaper over their heads - masthead on newspaper says "SUNDAY NEWS" and the paper shows black and white cartoons. A small pool of blue water under bench. Brown bird sitting on end of bench by boy and green frog with white eyes sitting on ground at other end of bench looking up at girl. Bench sitting on white base, top painted green as grass. Sculpted by Gerhard Bochmann. Color Variations: Also known with German headlines on newspaper. The original issue price was $26.00 in 1967. Price range: $200-250

Byj 52. **Skater's Waltz** (Skating "N" Dating): 4 1/2". Boy with red hair, wearing black and white checked shirt, green overalls, brown shoes, red handkerchief with black and white dots hanging from right rear pocket, left arm extended behind girl, right hand holding right hand of girl with red hair, red hair bow, wearing white coat lined in red in front and at sleeve cuffs, over a black and white checked dress, white petticoat, black hose, black and white shoes. Both figures on silver-wheeled roller skates, skating on white base, top painted as yellow and brown floor. Sculpted by Gerhard Bochmann. Color Variations: None known. The original issue price was $15.00 in 1967. Price range: $120-150

Byj 53. **Little Shopper** (Market Day): 4 1/4". Girl with red hair, red scarf with black dots at neck, wearing yellow blouse with black trim and long dark green pants, white sox, black shoes, holding loaf of French bread in left hand and green purse with red top with black dots on left arm. Right arm pushing silver wheeled shopping cart containing fresh vegetables. Off white cart has yellow edge trim and two yellow flowers and green leaves on side. Gray Schnauzer with red collar carrying white bone in mouth preceding girl. Both walking on white base, top painted yellow. Sculpted by Gerhard Bochmann. Color Variations: None known. The original issue price was $13.00 in 1967. Price range: $150-175

Byj 54. **Little Prayers Are Best:** 4 1/2". Girl with blonde hair, white scarf covering hair, wearing blue coat with black and white plaid patch on left coat hem, black stockings and shoes; kneeling at brown shrine. Shrine has figure with red crown, white gown with gold trim, covered by red coat. To her left on back edge of base is candelabra and at the front left edge of base is a basket of multicolored flowers, all resting on white base. Sculpted by Gerhard Skrobek. Color Variations: None known. The original issue price was $13.00 in 1966. Price range: $250-300

Byj 55. **Tender Shepherd:** 4 1/2". Boy with blonde hair, dressed in red robe with white shawl around shoulders, holding a black lamb to his chest, a white sheep standing to his right. Golden staff lying on white base, top painted as green grass. Sculpted by Gerhard Skrobek. Color Variations: None known. The original issue price was $8.00 in 1967. Price range: $250-300

Byj 56. **Her Shining Hour;** 7 1/2". Woman with blonde hair, wearing cream colored long dress with long sleeves, brown shoes, bending over slightly to hold both hands of child with blonde hair, wearing gold dressing gown, taking it's first steps on white base, top painted light green. Sculpted by Gerhard Skrobek. Color Variations: None known. The original issue price was $14.00 in 1966. Price range: $120-150

Byj 57. **Madonna Of The Doves:** 10 3/4". Woman with blonde hair, wearing blue gown, white sleeves showing from under gown, standing holding a small blonde child up to look into bird house on post. Bird house has gold roof, white bird looking out of house, white bird on roof, and two white birds lower on post and two birds at the base of post by the woman's foot. Green vine growing up post from ground. All standing on white base, top painted as green grass. Sculpted by Gerhard Skrobek. Color Variations: None known. The original issue price was $25.00 in 1967. Price range: $300-350

Byj 58M. **Rock A Bye Baby Music box:** *See Byj 37 for figurine description* .
Figurine mounted on dark brown stained revolving music box platform that
plays "Rock A Bye Baby" as it revolves. Sculpted by Gerhard Skrobek. Color
Variations: None known. The original issue price was $32.00 in 1968. Price
range: $300-350

Byj 59. **Little Prayers Are Best:** 4 1/2". Girl with brown/blonde hair, white scarf covering hair, wearing blue coat with blue and white plaid patch on left coat hem, black stockings and shoes, kneeling at brown shrine. Shrine has figure with red crown, white gown with gold trim, covered by red coat. To her left is tan basket containing multicolored flowers and all resting on white base. This figurine is the same as Byj 54, except, the candelabra has been removed from the left rear corner. Sculpted by Gerhard Skrobek. Color Variations: None known. The original issue price was $12.00 in 1968. Price range: $85-115

Byj 60. **Skater's Waltz Music Box:** *See Byj 52 for figurine description.*
Figurines mounted on dark brown stained revolving music box that plays
"Skaters Waltz" as it revolves. Sculpted by Gerhard Skrobek. Color Variations:
None known. The original issue price was $46.00 in 1968. Price range: $300-
350

Byj 61. **First Degree - Red hair:** 5 1/4". Girl with red hair, white mortar board hat with gold tassel on head, wearing white robe and shoes, holding white diploma tied with gold bow in right and left hands, a bouquet of six *yellow* roses with green stems laying across her arms. Girl standing on base painted gold. Sculpted by Gerhard Bochmann. Color Variations: None known. The original issue price was 18.00 in 1970. Price range: $70-95

Blonde hair: 5 1/4". Girl with dark blonde hair with white mortar board hat with brown tassel on head, wearing a white robe and brown shoes, holding white diploma tied with blue ribbon in right and left hands, a bouquet of six red roses with green stems laying across her arms. Girl standing on white base. Sculpted by Gerhard Bochmann. Color variations: None known. The original issue price was $41.00 in 1984. Price range: $60-75

Byj 62 **Swinger:** 5 1/4". Girl with long red hair, yellow flower bow and black headband, wearing white top trimmed in green, white pants decorated with green, yellow and red flowers, standing barefoot on white base, top painted green. Girl has green necklace matching green trim on top and strumming yellow guitar trimmed in black, red and green. Sculpted by Gerhard Bochmann. Color Variations: None known. The original issue price was $15.00 in 1970. Price range: $120-150

Byj 63. **Nurse - Red hair:** 5 1/4". Girl with red hair, wearing white nurse's cap, white uniform, stockings and shoes, holding a tan baby cradle containing multicolored flowers, standing on white base, top painted as black and white tiles. Sculpted by Gerhard Bochmann. Color Variations: None known. The original issue price was $13.00 in 1970. Price range: $70-95

Blonde hair:5 1/4". Girl with blonde hair, wearing white nurse's cap, white uniform, stockings and shoes, holding a tan baby cradle containing multicolored flowers, standing on white base, top molded as white tiles. Color Variations: None known. The original issue price was $49.00 in 1970. Price range: $60-75

Byj 64. **Love Bugs:** 7 1/2". Girl with long blonde hair, pink sunglasses in hair, wearing silver necklace, light pink long sleeved t-neck, pink long pants with patch on left knee, pink toenails, white sandals, left hand holding right hand of boy with brownish hair, wearing light blue t-neck, silver necklace, blue jean pants rolled up with hole in right knee, white sandals, left hand holding white guitar trimmed in pink and decorated with pink and blue designs. Both figurines standing on white base, top painted as green grass. Sculpted by Gerhard Skrobek. Color Variations: None known. The original issue price was $38 in 1968. Price range: $120-150

Byj 64M. **Love Bugs Music Box:** *See Byj 64 for figurine description.* Figurines mounted on dark brown stained revolving music box that plays "A Time To Remember" as it revolves. Sculpted by Gerhard Skrobek. Color variations: None known. The original issue price was $80.00 in 1970. Price range: $300-350

Byj 65. **Bongo Beat:** 4 1/4". Boy with red hair, wearing tan buckskin shirt and pants, red bracelet on left wrist, green bracelet on right wrist, red beads around neck, and white sandals with green strap on right foot and red straps on left foot, sitting on green and white plaid pillow playing two bongo drums in front of him. One drum green with black and white decorations, the other drum red with black and white decorations. Sculpted by Gerhard Skrobek. Color Variations: None known. The original issue price was $18.50 in 1970. Price range: $120-150

Byj 66. **Baby Sitter**: 5". Girl with red hair, black hair bow, wearing white t-neck with light brown and white striped sleeves, light green overalls, white shoes, sitting in off-white "scoop" type wicker chair, holding baby with blonde hair, white hair bow, in her lap, giving baby a bottle. At the right arm of girl is brown long eared toy rabbit with black eyes, nose and mouth. Chair sitting on brown bearskin rug; bear has black eyes, nose and mouth. Sculpted by Gerhard Skrobek. Color Variations: None known. The original issue price was $28.00 in 1970. Price range: $150-175

Byj 67. **Trouble Shooter - Red hair**: 5 1/2".
Boy with red hair, wearing black and white
checked shirt, green pants, white shoes, white
doctor's coat with red pencil in upper left
pocket and silver glasses in left lower pocket.
Right hand up on chest holding stethoscope and
left hand behind back holding large silver
hypodermic needle, standing on white base, top
painted as black and white tile floor. Sculpted
by Gerhard Skrobek. Color Variations: None
known. The original issue price was $13.00 in
1970. Price range: $70-95

This Won't Hurt - Blonde hair: As above but
boy has blonde hair and white base with
molded tile; base is all white. Sculpted by
Gerhard Skrobek. Color variations: None
known. The original issue price was $35.00 in
1970. Price range: $60-75

Byj 68. **Say A-aa-aah:** 5 3/8".
Boy with red hair, wearing
black and white checked shirt,
green pants, brown shoes, white
doctor's coat with yellow bone
in lower right pocket, holding
red pill in right hand and green
pill bottle with white cap in left
hand, about to administer a pill
to brownish, black and white
Basset hound type dog, bandage
on dog's tail with red cross on
bandage. Boy standing and dog
partially lying on white base
with molded white tile floor.
Sculpted by Gerhard Skrobek.
Color Variations: Known with
silver top on green pill bottle -
TMK 5. The original issue price
was $19.00 in 1970. Price
range: $120-150

Byj 69. **Bachelor Degree - Red hair:** 5 1/2". Boy with red hair, black mortar board hat on head, wearing white shirt, blue tie, black robe and shoes, right and left hands holding white diploma tied with blue ribbon, standing on gold base. Sculpted by Gerhard Skrobek. Color Variations: None known. The original issue price was $13.00 in 1970. Price range: $70-95

Brown hair: As above but boy has brown hair and white base. Sculpted by Gerhard Skrobek. Color Variations: None known. The original issue price was $49.00 in 1970. Price range: $60-75

Byj 70. **Lamp**: 8". tall lamp base. Birch tree trunk with Byj #6 **A Young Man's Fancy** 4 1/2". Girl with red hair, one green bow in hair, wearing orange dress with yellow polka dots, black hose, black and white shoes with red bow on side. Girl sitting on brown bench, looking down reading red book. Brown squirrel sitting on top left end of bench. Boy with red hair, wearing black and white checked shirt, green overalls and brown shoes, left hand holding bunch of yellow flowers, approaching girl from the right rear corner. Right hand on bench. Has green and yellow grass/flowers painted on white base. The primary difference in the Byj 6 figurine and the Byj 70 lamp is that there is a birch tree centered behind the bench on which the girl is sitting. Screw fittings for lamp at top of tree are evident. Prototype only other than prototype samples. Sculpted by Wittman. Price range: RARE

Byj 71. **Lamp**: 8". tall lamp base. Birch tree trunk with Byj #10 **Springtime** 4 1/2". Boy with red hair, wearing black and white checked shirt, green overalls with red patch and two white dots on seat of overalls, brown shoes, holding hammer with tan handle in left arm and white bird house with red roof in right arm, walking to birch tree trunk with two brown birds resting on top branch. Tree has green spots, as does the white base. The primary difference in the Byj 10 figurine and the Byj 71 lamp is that there is a birch tree centered with the boy holding hammer and birdhouse walking around base of tree which has two brown birds resting on sawed off limb. Screw type fittings for lamp at top of tree are evident. Prototype only other than prototype samples. Sculpted by Wittman. Price range: RARE

Byj 72. **Damper On The Camper** (New Friend): 4 1/2". Girl with red hair, head resting on green pillow, lying in yellow sleeping bag. Black and white skunk with tail raised standing on top of sleeping bag. Girl's left arm raised and clothed in red (white trimmed) pajama top. Green knapsack with tan straps and white buckles resting against end of sleeping bag as are blue shoes and white socks. Brown walking stick on ground to the left beside girl. Sleeping bag on white base, top painted as green grass. Sculpted by Gerhard Bochmann. Color Variations: None known. The original issue price was $75.00 in 1983. Price range: $175-200

Byj 73. **Heads Or Tails** (Concentration): 5 1/4". Boy with red hair, wearing green striped long sleeved and legged pajamas, bare footed, standing on his head. To his left is an open Yoga book and to his right is gray Schnauzer dog with black eyes, nose and mouth, trying to stand on floor on his own front feet. Both figures on white base, top painted tan color. Sculpted by Gerhard Bochmann. Color Variations: None known. The original issue price was $60.00 in 1983. Price range: $175-200

Byj 74. **Wash Day** (At Work) (Work Day): 4 3/4". Girl with red hair, black ribbon in hair, nude, sitting with left leg crossed over right leg, on blue and yellow box, reading book with green cover. In background is white clothes washer with black, red and green dials and silver trim around window/door with soap bubbles coming over top of machine and out window/door. Black electric cord appears from back of machine. Tan straw basket on floor with red and white sock over edge. All figures on white base. Sculpted by Gerhard Bochmann. Color Variations: None known. The original issue price was $55.00 in 1975. Price range: $175-200

Byj 75. **Sea Breeze:** 5". Girl with red hair, white sunglasses looking like life preservers with blue trim, wearing white top trimmed with blue at sleeves and neck, reclining in white deck chair trimmed in darker blue. Girl covered with white beach towel decorated around edge with red, red anchor in center of towel. Head of dachshund sticking out from under end of towel at her feet. Deck chair sitting on white base, top painted as tan and brown wooden deck. Sculpted by Gerhard Bochmann. Color Variations: None known. The original issue price was $65.00 in 1980. Price range: $175-200

Byj 76. **Barbecue:** 6 1/4". Boy with red hair, white chef's hat on head, wearing white t-neck, green overalls, white apron tied in back, black and white checks at bottom corners of apron, tan shoes, standing at light brown stone barbecue fireplace, red steak with white marbling on black grill, red handled barbecue tool with white trim under steak. Black cat with white feet, face, and tip of tail peering over top of barbecue fireplace, looking at steak. All figures standing on white base, top painted as green grass. Sculpted by Gerhard Skrobek. Color Variations: None known. The original issue price was $55.00 in 1976. Price range: $200-250

Byj 77. **1-2 Ski Doo** (Winning Team): 4 1/2". Girl with red hair, white hat on back of head, (top of hat painted green), white and black with matching neck scarf, wearing white t-neck and green sweater, white gloves with green trim at wrists sitting in and driving red snowmobile trimmed in black with blue windshield. Gray Schnauzer with black eyes, nose and red tongue, hanging out of left side of snowmobile. Top of base sculpted to look like snow. Sculpted by Gerhard Skrobek. Color Variations: None known. The original issue price was $75.00 in 1976. Price range: $175-200

Byj 78. **Lazy Day:** 5 1/4". Boy with red hair, yellow conical straw hat on head, red, black, white and green checked neckerchief at neck, wearing white long sleeved shirt trimmed in green on cuffs, green pants and white shoes, sitting, as though asleep, in red fishing boat trimmed in black, holding fishing pole in left hand. White can, silver lid, can decorated with white label with red apple with green stem sitting on boat seat to boy's right side. Boat oar sitting inside on boat seat. Gray Schnauzer with black eyes, nose and red mouth at front of boat leaning over edge, barking at another yellow paddle floating in blue water and silver fish outside the boat. White base, top painted as blue water. Sculpted by Gerhard Skrobek. Color Variations: None known. The original issue price was $55.00 in 1975. Price range: $200-250

Byj 79. **Camera Shy:** 6". Boy with red hair, standing, white sunglasses with silver lens on top of head, wearing white t-neck with red trim at neck and sleeves, green pants, silver flash attachment hanging from right rear pocket, white shoes, holding gray dog bone up in right hand while looking into black camera held in left hand. Boy has black camera case with brown carrying straps over left shoulder and tan camera bag at waist. Brown, black and white Basset type dog sitting between girl's legs. White base, top painted as green grass. Sculpted by Gerhard Skrobek. Color Variations: None known. The original issue price was $48.00 in 1975. Price range: $150-175

Byj 80. **Boy with Afghan Hound** - prototype only

Byj 81. **Condiment set** - prototype only

Byj 82. **Condiment set** - prototype only

Above: Byj 83. **Fore:** 4 3/4". Boy with red hair, leaning over, green golf cap on head, wearing yellow shirt with green tie, white sweater trimmed in black, yellow and white; gray pants, yellow sox, white shoes, holding black handled silver head gold club against white golf ball. To boy's left is tan golf bag with two silver golf clubs showing and gray Schnauzer, wearing white sweater standing on back feet against golf bag. All figures on white base, top painted as green grass. Sculpted by Gerhard Skrobek. Color Variations: None known. The original issue price was $48.00 in 1975. Price range: $150-175

Right: Byj 84. **Bird Watcher:** 5 1/4". Girl with long red hair, wearing yellow pith helmet with brown bird sitting on top of helmet, green sweater with white zigzag design across front, red, white and green plaid pants, black shoes, green bush at her feet. Girl's right hand holding black binoculars up to her eyes and red book with white pages held in her left hand at waist level. Girl standing on dark tan painted base. Sculpted by Gerhard Skrobek. Color Variations: None known. The original issue price was $48.00 in 1975. Price range: $150-175

Byj 85. **Captive Audience** (Wagtime Tune): 5". Boy with red hair, wearing black and white checked shirt, green overalls, white handkerchief hanging from left rear pocket, brown shoes, holding silver harmonica up close to mouth with right and left hands as white/gray dog with black eyes and nose sits listening on white base, top painted as green grass. Sculpted by Gerhard Skrobek. Color Variations: None known. The original issue price was $60.00 in 1982. Price range: $120-150

Byj 86. **Once Upon A Time:** 4 1/4". Girl with red hair, two green hair bows, wearing green dress trimmed in white at collar and sleeves, white apron with bow tied in back, white underpants trimmed in red and black, black hose, black and white shoes with red bows at sides and two black buttons on side of shoes. Girl sitting with red apple in right hand, open book on her lap with red cover, text reading "Once upon a time..." No base for this figurine. Sculpted by Gerhard Skrobek. Color Variations: None known. The original issue price was $55.00 in 1982. Price range: $120-150

Byj 87. **Four Letter Word For Ouch:** 4 1/2".
Boy with red hair, wearing black and white
checked shirt, green overalls, white shoes
trimmed in red, sitting on brown bench with
white papers visible under bench, holding
black and white crossword puzzle on lap and
red pencil in left hand. Right hand held up to
right cheek, large white cloth tied in a bow
knot on top of head. No base. Sculpted by
Gerhard Skrobek. Color Variations: None
known. The original issue price was $40.00 in
1982. Price range: $175-200

Byj 88. **Something Tells Me:** 5". Girl with red
hair, white hair bows, wearing lime green and
white plaid dress, white trim at sleeves and collar,
white underpants trimmed in red, black stockings,
black and white shoes with two black buttons and a
red bow. Girl counting fingers and standing on
white base, top painted green. Sculpted by Gerhard
Skrobek. Color Variations: None known. The
original issue price was $40.00 in 1982. Price
range: $175-200

Byj 89. **Yech!** (One Puffs Enough): 4 1/2".
Boy with red hair, wearing black and white
checked shirt, green overalls, white shoes,
standing with right hand on stomach, grimace
on his face. In left hand is large brown cigar
with white ash. To boy's left is red fire
hydrant. Boy and fire hydrant standing on
white base, top painted tan color. Sculpted by
Gerhard Skrobek. Color Variations: None
known. The original issue price was $55.00 in
1982. Price range: $150-175

Byj 90. **Nothing Beats A Pizza:** 4
1/2". Boy with red hair, wearing
green shirt, white overalls with
red handkerchief hanging from
right rear pocket, white tennis
shoes with red trim, carrying
pizza on white tray with white
napkin under pizza tray. Boy
walking on white base, top
painted light tan color. Sculpted
by Gerhard Skrobek. Color
Variations: None known. The
original issue price was $55.00 in
1982. Price range: $150-175

Byj 91. **A Funny Face From Outer Space:** 4 7/8". Boy with red hair, wearing white astronaut suit with silver buckles and holding helmet with right arm. Left arm around green pointed head alien with large eyes outlined in black, red nose and mouth and white hands. Both standing on white base, top painted tan color. Sculpted by Gerhard Skrobek. Color Variations: None known. The original issue price was $65.00 in 1982. Price range: $150-175

Byj 92. **Dear Sirs:** 5". Girl with red hair, two black hair bows and white glasses on head, wearing white blouse and jacket, black bow tie at neck, blue pleated skirt, black shoes with gray soles, sitting on book with yellow cover, holding blue pencil in right hand and white note pad in left hand on left knee crossed over right leg. Sculpted by Gerhard Skrobek. Color Variations: None known. The original issue price was $40.00 in 1982. Price range: $120-150

Byj 93. **Yeah Team:** 4 5/8". Boy with red hair, wearing light purple t-neck, sitting next to girl with red hair, white hair bow, wearing light purple t-neck, her white-gloved hand holding a red banner with white lettering "TEAM," a red thermos bottle with silver top sitting on floor between them. Green blanket with two black stripes surrounds boy and girl. No base on this figurine. Sculpted by Gerhard Skrobek. Color Variations: None known. The original issue price was $65.00 in 1982. Price range: $150-175

Byj 94. **Not Yet A Vet:** 4 1/2". Girl with red hair, black glasses up on head, along with white nurse's cap with red cross, wearing white nurse's uniform with scissors in left pocket, bandaging left front paw of orange tabby cat sitting on white medical chest with red cross on end of chest. Long brown dog with black eyes and nose, white bandage tied around his stomach, lies on base resembling a green tiled floor. Sculpted by Gerhard Skrobek. Color Variations: None known. The original issue price was $65.00 in 1982. Price range: $175-200

Byj 95. **Bedtime Boy:** 4 1/4". Boy with brown hair, wearing blue bathrobe with white trim at collar and sleeves, white house shoes, hands folded in front of his chest kneeling in prayer. No base on this figurine. Sculpted by Gerhard Skrobek. Color Variations: None known. The original issue price was $26.00 in 1984. Price range: $50-65

Byj 96. **Bedtime Girl**: 4". Girl with long blonde hair in ponytail, pink hair bow in back, wearing white nightgown with pink trim at collar and down the front, hands folded in front, bare feet, kneeling in prayer. No base on this figurine. Sculpted by Gerhard Skrobek. Color Variations: None known. The original issue price was $26.00 in 1984. Price range: $50-65

Byj 97. **Sweet Snack:** 3 3/4". Girl with short blonde hair, red hair bow with white dots, wearing blue dress with white lacelike trim at sleeves and red dots on white petticoat, red apron tied in back with white polka dots and white lacelike trim, pink stockings, white shoes, blue bows on sides, with tan soles. Right hand in jar labeled "JAM" in red and left hand with jam on fingers held up to her mouth. No base on this figurine. Sculpted by Gerhard Skrobek. Color Variations: None known. The original issue price was $42.00 in 1984. Price range: $60-75

Byj 98. **All Gone:** 4 1/4". Girl with brown hair in pigtails, blue hair bows, wearing blue pinafore over white dress, pink stockings, legs crossed left over right, white shoes with orange soles, sitting with gray spoon in right hand, eating from a tan bowl filled with brown pudding, held in lap with left hand. Sculpted by Gerhard Skrobek. Color Variations: None known. The original issue price was $40.00 in 1984. Price range: $60-75

Byj 99. **Sharing Secrets:** 5 1/2". Boy with blonde hair, wearing tan shirt with orange and brown stripes, light blue overalls, brown shoes with tan soles, lying on stomach on white base, top painted as green grass with yellow flowers with black centers, looking at and talking to yellow duck with orange bill and black eyes. Sculpted by Gerhard Skrobek. Color Variations: As above but with white shirt with brown and orange stripes. The original issue price was $44.00 in 1984. Price range: $85-115

Byj 100. **Farm Friends:** 4 7/8". Girl with brown hair, orange scarf over head tied under chin, wearing blue dress with white trim at collar and bottom edge of dress, white apron over dress, bow in back, white petticoat showing, brown shoes, holding multicolored bouquet of flowers with green stems in left hand and right hand resting on shoulder of a white sheep with black eyes, nose and mouth. Both figurines standing on white base, top painted as green grass. Sculpted by Gerhard Skrobek. Color Variations: As above but lamb without black nose and mouth. The original issue price was $46.00 in 1984. Price range: $120-150

Byj 101. **Come Along:** 3 7/8". Boy with blonde hair, wearing reddish/orange shirt, blue jean pants, brown shoes, light green knapsack with black shoulder straps and trim on back, with cream colored bedroll under knapsack, holding brown flute in right and left hands as he walks on white base, top painted as green grass. Sculpted by Gerhard Skrobek. Color Variations: None known. The original issue price was $47.50 in 1985. Price range: $120-150

Byj 102. **Please Wait:** 3 1/8". Girl with blonde hair, flower in right side of hair, wearing white sweater with orange trim at neck and edge of sleeves, blue jean pants, brown shoes, and golden orange knapsack with black shoulder straps, sitting on stump resting, and looking to the right, with left hand up to left ear and right hand on brown tree stump, two white flowers around base of stump on white base, top painted as green grass. Sculpted by Gerhard Skrobek. Color Variations: As above but with blue flowers with black centers. The original issue price was $47.50 in 1985. Price range: $120-150

Byj 103. **Staying Fit:** 5". Boy with red hair, wearing white sweat suit trimmed in green at neck, on sleeves and around sleeve cuffs and outside edge of white pants, black shoes trimmed with white. Across front of sweatshirt lettered "Jogger" in black letters. On white base, top painted as green grass. Sculpted by Gerhard Skrobek. Color Variations: None known. The original issue price was $45.00 in 1985. Price range: $120-150

Byj 104. **Almost There**: 5". Girl with red hair, green hair bows, white sweat band on head, wearing white sweat suit trimmed in red at neck, on sleeves and around sleeve cuffs and outside edge of white pants, black shoes trimmed in white. Across front of sweatshirt lettered "Jogger" in black letters. On white base, top painted as green grass. Sculpted by Gerhard Skrobek. Color Variations: None known. The original issue price was $45.00 in 1985. Price range: $120-150

Byj 105. **The Collector:** 2 7/8". Girl with red hair, two white hair bows, wearing white sweater trimmed in light blue at collar and edge of sleeves, light blue pants, white shoes, kneeling, looking at and holding black, red and green doll in hands. To her right is small three level white cabinet with two shelves, each holding two painted dolls, and one doll with blonde hair wearing red robe trimmed in white standing on top of cabinet. All figurines on white base, top painted as tan floor. Sculpted by Gerhard Skrobek. Color Variations: None known. The original issue price was $64.00 in 1985. Price range: $300-350

Byj 106. **The Practice:** 2 7/8". Girl with red hair, green hair bow, wearing mustard colored dress with white trim at collar and bottom of dress, red trim at sleeves, black hose, black and white shoes with red bow and black button on side of shoes, sitting down with legs apart playing white piano with black and white keys as brownish/gray kitten with pink ears and black eyes sits on back legs with front legs on top of piano listening and looking at girl. No base on this figurine. Sculpted by Gerhard Skrobek. Color Variations: None known. The original issue price was $64.00 in 1985. Price range: $300-350

Byj 107. **Shall We Dance:** 4 1/8". Girl angel with blonde hair, wearing light blue nightgown trimmed in white at collar and edge of sleeves, yellow shoes, white wings on her back, holding hands and dancing with dark brown teddy bear with blue bow at neck and silver windup key on side, on white base molded as cloud. Sculpted by Gerhard Skrobek. Color Variations: None known. The original issue price was $72.50 in 1986. Price range: $200-250

Byj 108. **Greetings:** 4 3/4". Girl angel with blonde hair, pink star in hair, white wings on back trimmed in light blue at ends, wearing pink gown, feet bare, holding gold and black banner with red "GREETINGS" lettered on white background, standing on white base. Sculpted by Gerhard Skrobek. Color Variations: None known. The original issue price was $55.00 in 1986. Price range: $200-250

Byj 109. **A Special Friend:** 4 1/4". Black girl angel, black hair, blue hair bow, white wings trimmed in blue on back, wearing blue gown, feet bare, holding white kitten in left arm and sitting on white base molded as a cloud. Sculpted by Gerhard Skrobek. Color Variations: None known. The original issue price was $55.00 in 1986. Price range: $200-250

Byj 110. **Communion:** 4 3/4". Blonde girl, white hair covering on back of head, blue eyes, red mouth wearing full length white first communion dress with long sleeves. White bible with cross in left hand and white and green flowers in left arm. White candles with red top and silver ribbon held in right hand. Sculpted by Gerhard Skrobek. Prototype only.

BYJ ALPHABETICAL LISTING

I find it extremely useful to have a listing of all of Byj figurines in alphabetical order. This enables me to easily determine the Byj number if I am using a checklist or comparing color variations. I hope that you too will find this listing useful.

Byj 17. A Child's Prayer
Byj 91. A Funny Face From Outer Space
Byj 109. A Special Friend
Byj 6. A Young Man's Fancy
Byj 98. All Gone
Byj 104. Almost There
Byj 7. Atta Boy

Byj 66. Baby Sitter
Byj 69. Bachelor Degree, Red hair #5279; Brown hair #5402
Byj 76. Barbeque
Byj 95. Bedtime Boy
Byj 96. Bedtime Girl
Byj 84. Bird Watcher
Byj 16. Bless Us All
Byj 42. Bless Us All - Lamp
Byj 65. Bongo Beat
Byj 80. Boy with Afghan - prototype only

Byj 29. Calorie Counter - (Wall Plaque)
Byj 79. Camera Shy
Byj 85. Captive Audience
Byj 50. Cheer Up
Byj 101. Come Along
Byj 110. Communion
Byj 81. Condiment set - prototype only
Byj 82. Condiment set - prototype only
Byj 48. Copper Topper

Byj 24. Daisies Won't Tell
Byj 72. Damper On The Camper
Byj 47. Dealer Display Plaque
Byj 92. Dear Sirs
Byj 45. Dropping In

Byj 9. E-e-eek
Byj 38. Evening Prayer

Byj 100. Farm Friends
Byj 61. First Degree, Red hair #5278; Brown hair #540
Byj 20. Forbidden Fruit
Byj 83. Fore
Byj 87. Four Letter Word For Ouch

Byj 28. Gangway
Byj 31. Gingerbread boy & girl salt & pepper shakers & sled as tray

Byj 30. Girl bust salt shaker - Muff as pepper shaker and separate tray
Byj 26. Good News
Byj 108. Greetings
Byj 40. Guess Who

Byj 73. Heads Or Tails
Byj 56. Her Shining Hour

Byj 43. Just Hitched - (Wall Plaque)

Byj 70. Lamp - Birch tree trunk - with Byj #6 (Young Man's Fancy) - prototype only
Byj 71. Lamp - Birch tree trunk - with Byj #10 (Springtime) - prototype only
Byj 78. Lazy Day
Byj 51. Let It Rain
Byj 4. Little Miss Coy
Byj 54. Little Prayers Are Best
Byj 59. Little Prayers Are Best (revised Byj 54)
Byj 53. Little Shopper
Byj 64. Love Bugs
Byj 64M. Love Bugs (Music Box)
Byj 44. Lucky Day

Byj 57. Madonna Of The Doves
Byj 21. Moon Light Sonata (Plaque)
Byj 36. Mother Embracing Child

Byj 94. Not Yet A Vet
Byj 90. Nothing Beats A Pizza
Byj 63. Nurse, Red hair #5281; Blonde hair #5403

Byj 22. Off Key
Byj 8. O'Hair For President
Byj 34. Old Man Street Cleaner
Byj 86. Once Upon A Time
Byj 77. 1-2 Ski Doo
Byj 3. Oops

Byj 102. Please wait
Byj 27. Plenty Of Nothing
Byj 41. Pretzel Lena
Byj 25. Putting On The Dog

Byj 37. Rock A Bye Baby
Byj 58M. Rock A Bye Baby (Music Box)

Byj 68. Say A-aa-aah
Byj 75. Sea Breeze
Byj 107. Shall We Dance
Byj 99. Sharing Secrets
Byj 5. Shear Nonsense
Byj 12. Sitting Pretty
Byj 52. Skater's Waltz
Byj 60M. Skater's Waltz (Music Box)
Byj 11. Sleepy Head
Byj 88. Something Tells Me
Byj 19. Spellbound
Byj 35. Spring Cleaning
Byj 10. Springtime
Byj 32. Standing man & woman (salt & pepper shakers)
Byj 15. Starling (wall plaque)
Byj 103. Staying Fit
Byj 1. Strike
Byj 39. Super Service
Byj 97. Sweet Snack

Byj 62. Swinger

Byj 55. Tender Shepherd
Byj 105. The Collector
Byj 23. The Kibitzer
Byj 106. The Practice
Byj 2. The Roving Eye
Byj 18. The Stolen Kiss
Byj 46. The Way To Pray
Byj 49. Trim Lass
Byj 67. Trouble Shooter, Red hair #5283; Blonde hair #5410

Byj 33. Upside down umbrella candy dish

Byj 74. Wash Day

Byj 93. Yeah Team
Byj 89. Yech!

CHARLOT BYJ CHRISTMAS PLATES

701 1973 Annual Christmas Plate: 8 1/2". diameter. Santa sitting on white chair, placing toys under Christmas tree, Schnauzer puppy tugging at his pants while three redheaded children with kittens watch in the background. Green and red stocking at top of plate bears the message "1973 Happy Holidays." The original issue price was $21.00 in 1973. Color variations: None known. Price range: $25-40

703 **1974 Annual Christmas Plate:** 8 1/2". diameter. Blonde girl, blue hair bow, wearing blue nightgown, kneeling and hugging Santa Claus who is dressed in traditional red and white Santa suit.. Christmas tag on Santa's coat bears the message "Happy Holiday 1974." The original issue price was $29.50 in 1974. Color variations: None known. Price range: $25-40

705 **1975 Annual Christmas Plate:** 8 1/2". diameter. Girl angel, red hair, white wings, wearing blue nightgown with red bow at neck, leaning against white pillow which is placed against yellow crescent shaped moon as bed, watching Santa Claus and reindeer fly through the sky. Girl covered with red patchwork quilt. Bird sitting on bottom end of moon. Santa's toy sack dropping toys as they fly, message on toy sack "Happy Holiday 1975." The original issue price was $29.50 in 1975.Color variations: None known. Price range: $25-40

706 **1976 Annual Christmas Plate:** 8 1/2". diameter. Boy with red hair, wearing red pajamas, kneeling on floor, hugging a brown teddy bear which has a green bow at the neck and red, white and green candy cane around the left wrist. Child's "green" board in background has message "Happy Holiday 1976." The original issue price was $29.50 in 1976. Color variations: None known. Price range: $25-40

707 **1977 Annual Christmas Plate:** 8 1/2". diameter. Boy with red hair, wearing gold t-neck sweater and green overalls looking down at Baby Jesus in red straw filled manger being held by girl with long blonde hair, red hair bow. Girl wearing white top decorated with green holly leaves and red holly berries. "1977" at bottom center of plate. The original issue price was $29.50 in 1977. Color variations: None known. Price range: $25-40

1975 Limited Edition Pewter Plate 9". diameter - Girl kneeling, same as Byj 16, on cushion under her knees, baby bed appears to the left edge of plate. Girl has stars on her gown. Charlot Byj name appears to the lower right edge on face of plate. Color variations: None known. Price range: $40-60

1979 White satin ball with red and green holly around upper part of ball; "Rock-a-bye-Baby Merry Christmas 1979" printed in blue around center of ball. Byj 37 - Rock-a-bye Baby figurine also featured on ball. The original issue price in 1979 unknown. Price range: $10-15

1979 White satin ball with red and green holly around upper part of ball: "Merry Christmas Nurse 1979" printed in red. Byj 63 - Red headed nurse also featured on ball. The original issue price in 1979 unknown. Price range: $10-15

no photo

1980 White satin ball with red and green holly around the upper part of ball: "Merry Christmas nurse 1980" printed in red. Byj 63 – Red headed nurse also featured on ball. The original issue price in 1980 unknown. Price range: $10-15

no photo

1980 White satin ball with Merry Christmas around upper part of ball. Snow scene with Byj 52 Skater's Waltz design and dated 1980 in lower right portion of scene. The original issue price in 1980 unknown. Price range: $10-15

9201 **Baby in Stocking Ornament** (1986): Blonde infant wearing cerise sleepers, head on white pillow trimmed in green on edges, resting in large red stocking marked "HANDLE WITH CARE" in black letters on lower front and "FRAGILE" in white letters on left side of stocking. Hole in top of stocking suitable for hanging. Marked on back in black "Goebel W.Germany 1985. Sculpted by Gerhard Skrobek. Sculpted by Gerhard Skrobek. The original issue price in 1986 was $18.00. Price range: $15-30

9202 **Baby In Snow-Dress Ornament** (1987): Small child wearing red snowsuit, blond hair showing from under red cap trimmed in white around face, with sprig of green holly with red berry in center on trim. Hat has white tip on end; red candy cane in child's left rear pocket, brown shoes, carrying in white mittened hands a gift with green ribbon and red berry in center. Brass loop from top of head suitable for hanging. Bottom of right foot marked "Goebel - WGermany 1986." Bottom left foot incised "60." Sculpted by Gerhard Skrobek. The original issue price in 1987 was $20.00. Price range: $15-30

no photo

9203 **Child In Stocking Ornament** (1988): *(not shown)* Child with blonde hair, red poinsettia on right front of hair, wearing blue sleepers, looking to it's right as it sits in red Christmas stocking striped with white and gold over the white. Hole in top of stocking suitable for hanging. Sculpted by Gerhard Skrobek. The original issue price in 1988 was $27.50. Price range: $15-30

9204 **Baby In Boot Ornament** (1989): Boy angel, white wings tipped in black on back, black hair, blue sweater trimmed in white at sleeves, holding a green horn in both hands, standing in large red boot with bow on right side outlined in black. Brass loop on head suitable for hanging. Marked on bottom of boot in black Goebel W. Germany 1988. Sculpted by Gerhard Skrobek. The original issue price in 1989 is unknown. Price range: $15-30

101060 **Baby In Sled Ornament** (1990): Child with brown hair, wearing red cap trimmed in white with black accents, red coat, white muff with red bow and gold bells, sitting in greenish sled with "1990" in black letters on left side, red blanket with green and white patches. Brass loop on top suitable for hanging. Marked in blue "Goebel - Germany – 1989." Sculpted by Gerhard Skrobek. The original issue price in 1990 was $30.00. Price range: $15-30

101061 **Baby In Moon Ornament** (1991): Girl angel with gray wings, black hair rolled with cloth bows, head resting on white pillow trimmed in blue, wearing white pajamas with orchid stars, bare feet, asleep on yellow crescent shaped moon marked "1991." in gray on left side, alarm clock on left side of moon on floor -time is 7:00; blue house shoes on floor on left side of moon and white chamber pot on right side of moon. Hole in upper part of moon with gold tinsel cord suitable for hanging. Marked in blue ink "Goebel - Germany - 1989" on lower right side of moon. Sculpted by Gerhard Skrobek. The original issue price in 1991 was $35.00. Price range: $15-30

9101 **"St. Lucia" Christmas Bell** (1986): Girl, long blonde hair, wearing light green hat trimmed in darker green, white robe, red ribbon around neck, holding green candle with yellow and red flame in front of her. Brass ring in top suitable for hanging. Marked "1986" and "Goebel - WGermany 1985" in blue inside bell. Sculpted by Gerhard Skrobek. The original issue price in 1986 was $18.00. Price range: $15-30

9102 **"Boy Angel Holding Star" Christmas Bell** (1987): Boy angel with blonde hair, green wreath with red berries on head, holding orange star in right hand, wearing white robe, brown shoes, green pants showing in back. Brass ring in top suitable for hanging. Marked "1987" and "Goebel - WGermany - 1986" in blue inside bell. Sculpted by Gerhard Skrobek. The original issue price in 1987 was $20.00. Price range: $15-30

no photo

9103 **"Girl Angel With Music Book" Christmas Bell** (1988): *(not shown)* Girl angel with long blonde hair, white wings, wearing white robe, both hands in front holding green music scroll. Brass ring in top suitable for hanging. Marked "1988" and "Goebel - WGermany 1988" in blue inside bell. Sculpted by Gerhard Skrobek. The original issue price in 1988 was $22.50. Price range: $15-30

9104 **"Girl Angel Holding Candle" Christmas Bell** (1989): Girl with black hair, black hat trimmed in white with red bows, wearing white robe trimmed in very light blue, holding red flower-yellow center - green stem in right arm and red candle with yellow flame in left hand. Reddish brown shoe. Brass ring in top suitable for hanging. Marked "1989" and "Goebel - WGermany 1987" in blue inside of bell. Sculpted by Gerhard Skrobek. The original issue price in 1989 is unknown. Price range: $15-30

APPENDIX: ROCKY ROCKHOLT QUICK LISTING

The following comprises a complete listing of Charlot Byj designed products that were produced by Goebel Porzellanfabrik. The purpose of the "Quick List" is to enable a collector to quickly identify any item the has been produced by Goebel..

ITEM DESCRIPTION	SIZE	U. S. No.	MOLD No.	MOLD DATE	INITIAL PRICE	INTRO /RETIRE	SCULPTOR	KNOWN TDM'S
Byj 1 Strike	4"	5251	10001-01-4	1957	6.00	1957/86	Moeller	3, 4, 5, 6
Boy with bowling ball								
Byj 2 The Roving Eye	4 1/2"	5252	10002-01-2	1957	6.00	1957/86	Skrobek	3, 4, 5, 6
Boy winking with puppy								
Byj 3 Oops	4 3/4"	5253	10003-01-0	1957	8.00	1957/88	Moeller	3, 4, 5, 6
Girl with three kittens								
Byj 4 Little Miss Coy	4 1/2"	5254	10004-01-8	1957	6.00	1957/86	Skrobek	3, 4, 5, 6
Shy girl with straw hat								
Byj 5 Shear Nonsense (Make It Short)	5"	5255	10005-01-5	1957	10.00	1957/86	Moeller	3, 4, 5, 6
Boy cutting girl's hair								
Byj 6 A Young Man's Fancy	4 1/2"	5256	10006-01-3	1957	10.00	1957/88	Moeller	3, 4, 5, 6
Girl on bench-boy with flowers								
Byj 7 Atta Boy (Howdy)	4"	5257	10007-01-1	1958	6.50	1958/85	Moeller	3, 4, 5, 6
Boy training his dog								
Byj 8 O'Hair For President (Lend Me Your Ears)	5 1/4"	5258	10008-01-9	1957	6.00	1957/83	Skrobek	3, 4, 5, 6
Boy on soap box								
Byj 9 E-ee-eek	4 1/2"	5259	10009-01-7	1957	8.00	1957/86	Skrobek	3, 4, 5, 6
Girl with puppy tugging her pants								
Byj 10 Springtime (Dreamhouse)	4 1/2"	5260	10010-01-5	1957	7.50	1957/83	Skrobek	3, 4, 5, 6
Boy with birdhouse								
Byj 11 Sleepy Head (Blonde)	5 1/2"	5351	10011-01-3	1957	9.00	1957/82	Moeller	3, 4, 5, 6
Boy yawning with Teddy bear								
Byj 12 Sitting Pretty (Blonde)	5"	5261	10012-01-1	1957	9.00	1957/83	Moeller	3, 4, 5, 6
Girl with straw hat & flowers								
Byj 13 Open Number								
Byj 14 Open Number								
Byj 15 Starling Plaque (Blonde)	4 1/2" x 6"		10015-01-0	1957		1957/60	Mensenbach	3, 4
Boy angel sitting on cloud								
Byj 16 Bless Us All (Blonde)	5 1/4"	5352	10016-01-2	1957	6.00	1957/83	Mensenbach	3, 4, 5, 6
Boy kneeling in prayer								
Byj 17 A Child's Prayer (Blonde)	5 1/4"	5353	10017-01-2	1957	6.00	1957/83	Mensenbach	3, 4, 5, 6
Girl kneeling in prayer								

ITEM	DESCRIPTION	SIZE	U.S. No.	MOLD No.	MOLD DATE	INITIAL PRICE	INTRO /RETIRE	SCULPTOR	KNOWN TDM'S
Byj 18	The Stolen Kiss *Redhead boy & blonde girl*	5 1/2"		10018-01-8	1957	13.00	1957/79	Moeller	3, 4, 5, 6
Byj 19	Spellbound *Girl sitting at desk reading*	5 1/2"	5263	10019-01-6	1958	12.00	1958/88	Wolf	3, 4, 5, 6
Byj 20	Forbidden Fruit *Boy with apples*	4 1/4"		10020-01-4	1958	7.00	1958/79	Wolf	3, 4, 5
Byj 21	Moon Light Sonata (Moonshine Sonata)Plaque *Boy & girl on rooftop*	4 3/4" x 5"					1958/60	Wehlt/Byj	3, 4
Byj 22	Off Key *Boy on chair with banjo*	5 1/2"	5264	10022-01-0	1958	7.50	1958/83	Mensenbach	3, 4
Byj 23	The Kibitzer *The story teller & dog*	4 3/4"	5265	10023-01-8	1958	7.50	1958/83	Mensenbach	3, 4, 5
Byj 24	Daisies Won't Tell *Girl picking flowers*	4 1/4"	5266	10024-01-6	1956	6.00	1957/85	Skrobek	3, 4, 5, 6
Byj 25	Putting On The Dog *Girl walking with two dogs*	5"	5267	10025-01-3	1956	9.00	1957/85	Skrobek	3, 4, 5, 6
Byj 26	Good News *Boy with flowers & candy*	4 1/2"	5268	10026-01-1	1958	6.00	1958/88	Mensenbach	3, 4, 5, 6
Byj 27	Plenty Of Nothing *Boy with empty pockets*	4 1/4"	5269	10027-01-9	1958	5.50	1958/88	Wehlt	3, 4, 5, 6
Byj 28	Gangway *Boy & puppy on go cart*	4 1/2"	5270	10028-01-7	1958	8.50	1958/88	Wehlt	3, 4, 5, 6
Byj 29	Calorie Counter Plaque *Fat lady on stool at counter*	3 3/4" x 7"			None		1958/60	Wagner	3
Byj 30	Girl, Muff & Tray as Salt & Pepper Shaker	3 1/2"			1959		1959/60	Wolf	3
Byj 31	Gingerbread Boy, Girl & Sled as Salt & Pepper Shaker	3 1/2"			1959		1959/61	Wolf	3
Byj 32	Standing Man & Woman as Salt & Pepper Shaker	3 1/2"			1959		1959/61	Wehlt	3
Byj 33	Upside down Umbrella Candy Dish	5"			1959		1959/60	Naumann	3
Byj 34	Old Man Street Cleaner as Toothbrush Holder	5 1/2"			1959		1959/60	Wagner	3
Byj 35	Spring Cleaning *Woman With Broom as Pencil Holder*	5 1/2"			1959		1959/60	Wagner	3
Byj 36	Mother Embracing Child (Blonde) *Kneeling mother & child*	8 1/2"	5354	10036-01-0	1959	7.50	1959/88	Skrobek	3, 4, 5, 6
Byj 37	Rock-A-By-Baby (Blonde) *Girl swinging baby on knee*	6 1/4"	5355	10037-01-8	1959	8.00	1959/88	Skrobek	3, 4, 5, 6
Byj 38	Evening Prayer (Blonde) *Girl & doll kneeling in prayer*	6 1/4"	5356	10038-01-6	1959	8.50	1959/88	Skrobek	3, 4, 5, 6

ITEM DESCRIPTION	SIZE	U.S. No.	MOLD No.	MOLD DATE	INITIAL PRICE	INTRO /RETIRE	SCULPTOR	KNOWN TDM'S
Byj 39 Super Service *Boy taking grocery order*	5 1/4"		10039-01-4	1959	9.00	1959/79	Moeller	3, 4, 5, 6
Byj 40 Guess Who *Boy pulling girl's hair*	5"		10040-01-2	1958	8.50	1959/79	Moeller	3, 4, 5
Byj 41 Pretzel Lena *Girl standing in front of tray*	3 3/4"		10041	1958		1958/59	Wagner	3
Byj 42 Evening Prayer Night lamp With Byj 38	4 1/2" x 4 3/4"					1963/63	Skrobek	4
Byj 43 Just Hitched Plaque *Honeymoon couple in car*			10043	1963		1963/63	Bochmann	4
Byj 44 Lucky Day *Boy finding 4 leaf clover*	3"	5271	10044-01-4	1963	5.50	1963/88	Bochmann	3, 4, 5, 6
Byj 45 Dropping In *Girl with flowers*	5"	5272	10045-01-1	1963	6.00	1963/88	Bochmann	3, 4, 5, 6
Byj 46 The Way To Prayer (Blonde) *Girl showing boy how to hold hands in prayer*	4 1/4"	5357	10046-01-9	1963	8.50	1963/88	Bochmann	3, 4, 5, 6
Byj 47 Byj Dealer Plaque *Byj 4 and Goebel signing*	4 1/2"	5273	10047	1966	4.00	1966/88	Skrobek	3, 4, 5, 6
Byj 48 Copper Topper (Forward March) *Girl with pot on head*	4 3/4"	5274	10048-01-5	1967	10.00	1967/88	Bochmann	3, 4, 5
Byj 49 Trim Lass *Girl mowing lawn*	4 1/2"		10049-01-3	1967	14.00	1967/78	Bochmann	4, 5
Byj 50 Cheer Up *Nurse holding fruit basket*	5"	5275	10050-01-1	1967	8.00	1967/88	Bochmann	4, 5, 6
Byj 51 Let It Rain *Boy & girl with newspaper over their heads*	6"	5276	10051-01-9	1957	26.00	1967/88	Bochmann	4, 5, 6
Byj 52 Skater's Waltz (Skatin "N" Datin) *Girl & boy roller skating*	4 1/2"	5277	10052-01-7	1957	15.00	1967/79	Bochmann	4, 5, 6
Byj 53 Little Shopper (Market Day) *Girl & dog with grocery cart*	4 1/4"		10053-01-5	1957	13.00	1967/78	Bochmann	4, 5
Byj 54 Little Prayers Are Best (Blonde) *Girl praying at shrine*	4 1/2"	5360	10054		13.00	1966/68	Skrobek	4
Byj 55 Tender Shepherd (Blonde) *Boy with sheep & red robe*	4 1/2"		10055-01-0	1967	8.00	1967/74	Skrobek	4, 5
Byj 56 Her Shining Hour (Blonde) *Mother hold baby as it walks*	7 1/2"	5358	10056-01-8	1966	14.00	1966/88	Skrobek	4, 5, 6
Byj 57 Madonna Of The Doves (Blonde) *Madonna holding baby watching doves*	10 3/4"	5359	10057-01-6	1967	25.00	1967/88	Skrobek	4, 5, 6
Byj 58M Rock-A-Bye-Baby (Music box) *Music box with Byj 37*	8 1/4"	5355	10058-01-4	MB	32.00	1968/80 In 1973	Skrobek	4

ITEM DESCRIPTION	SIZE	U.S. No.	MOLD No.	MOLD DATE	INITIAL PRICE	INTRO /RETIRE	SCULPTOR	KNOWN TDM'S
Byj 59 Little Prayers Are Best (Blonde) *Restyled Byj 54*	4 1/2"	5360	10059-	1967	12.00	1968/88	Skrobek	4,5
Byj 60M Skater's Waltz (Music box) *Music box with Byj 52*	8 1/4"		10060-01-0	MB	46.00 In 1973	1968/80	Skrobek	4, 5, 6
Byj 61 First Degree (Redhead)	5 1/4"	5278	10060-01-0	1970	18.00	1970/88	Bochmann	4, 5, 6
Byj 61 First Degree (Brown) *Girl graduate with flowers*	5 1/4"	5401	10061-01-8		49.00	1984/88	Bochmann	4, 5, 6
Byj 62 Swinger *Girl with guitar*	5 1/4"	5280	10062-01-6	1970	15.00	1970/83	Bochmann	4, 5, 6
Byj 63 Nurse (Redhead)	5 1/4"	5281	10063	1970	13.00	1970/88	Bochmann	4, 5, 6
Byj 63 Nurse (Brown) *Nurse holding basket of flowers*	5 1/4"	5403	10063-11-3	1970	49.00	1984/88	Bochmann	4, 5, 6
Byj 64 Love Bugs (Blonde) *Boy & girl holding hands*	7 1/2"		10064-01-2	1970	38.00	1970/79	Skrobek	4
Byj 64M Love Bugs (Music Box) *Music box with Byj 64*	9 1/2"		10064-21-0	1970	80.00	1970/80	Skrobek	5
Byj 65 Bongo Beat *Boy with bongo drums*	4 1/4"		10065-01-9	1970	18.50	1970/80	Skrobek	4, 5
Byj 66 Baby Sitter *Girl giving baby a bottle*	5"	5282	10066-01-7	1970	28.00	1970/83	Skrobek	4, 5
Byj 67 Trouble Shooter (Redhead)	5 1/2"	5283	10067-01-5	1970	13.00	1970/86	Skrobek	4, 5, 6
Byj 67 This Won't Hurt (Brown) *Doctor hiding needle*	5 1/2"	5410	10067-11-0	1970		1970/86	Skrobek	4, 5, 6
Byj 68 Say A-aa-aah *Boy playing vet with dog*	5 3/8"	5284	10068-01-3	1970	19.00	1970/86	Skrobek	4, 5, 6
Byj 69 Bachelor Degree (Redhead)	5 1/2"	5279	10069-01-1	1970	18.00	1970/88	Skrobek	4, 5, 6
Byj 69 Bachelor Degree (Brown) *Boy graduating*	5 1/2"	5402	10069-11-0	1970	49.00	1984/88	Skrobek	4, 5, 6
Byj 70L Lamp: Birch Tree Trunk with Byj 6 (Young Man's Fancy)	8"						Wittman	Prototype
Byj 71L Lamp: Birch Tree Trunk with Byj 10 (Springtime)	8"						Wittman	Prototype
Byj 72 Damper On The Camper (New Friend) *Girl in sleeping bag & skunk*	4 1/2"	5291	10072-01-5	1980	75.00	1983/86	Bochmann	6
Byj 73 Heads Or Tails (Concentration) *Boy & dog doing headstand*	5 1/4"	5292	10073-01-3	1980	60.00	1983/86	Bochmann	6
Byj 74 Wash Day (Work Day) *Girl washing her clothes*	4 3/4"	5285	10074-01-1	1975	55.00	1975/86	Bochmann	4, 5, 6
Byj 75 Sea Breeze *Girl sitting in deck chair*	5"	5293	10075-01-8	1980	65.00	1980/86	Bochmann	4, 5, 6
Byj 76 Barbeque *Boy in chefs hat*	6 1/4"	5286	10076-01-6	1976	55.00	1975/83	Skrobek	4, 5, 6

ITEM	DESCRIPTION	SIZE	U.S. No. 5294	MOLD No. 10077-01-4	MOLD DATE 1976	INITIAL PRICE 75.00	INTRO /RETIRE 1976/86	SCULPTOR Skrobek	KNOWN TDM'S 6
Byj 77	1-2 Ski Doo (Winning Team) *Girl & dog in snowmobile*	4 1/2"	5294	10077-01-4	1976	75.00	1976/86	Skrobek	6
Byj 78	Lazy Day *Boy in rowboat*	5 1/4"	5287	10078-01-2	1975	55.00	1975/86	Skrobek	5, 6
Byj 79	Camera Shy *Girl taking pictures*	6"	5288	10079-01-0	1975	48.00	1975/83	Skrobek	5, 6
Byj 80	Boy With Afghan Hound							Skrobek	Prototype
Byj 81	Condiment Set							Skrobek	Prototype
Byj 82	Condiment Set							Skrobek	Prototype
Byj 83	Fore *Boy golfer*	4 3/4"	5289	10083-01-2	1975	48.00	1975/83	Skrobek	6
Byj 84	Bird Watcher *Girl with field glasses*	5 1/4"	5270	10084-01-0	1975	48.00	1975/83	Skrobek	6
Byj 85	Captive Audience (Wagtime Tune) *Boy with harmonica*	5"	5305	10085-01-7	1982	55.00	1982/88	Skrobek	6
Byj 86	Once Upon A Time (Fairy Tales) *Girl eating apple & reading*	4 1/4"	5306	10086-01-5	1982	55.00	1982/88	Skrobek	6
Byj 87	Four Letter Word For Ouch *Boy with toothache*	4 1/2"	5295	10087-01-3	1982	40.00	1982/88	Skrobek	6
Byj 88	Something Tells Me *Girl counting her fingers*	5"	5299	10088-01-3	1982	40.00	1982/88	Skrobek	6
Byj 89	Yech (One Puffs Enough) *Boy smoking cigar*	4 1/2"	5308	10089-01-9	1982	55.00	1982/88	Skrobek	6
Byj 90	Nothing Beats A Pizza *Boy holding a pizza*	4 1/2"	5296	10090-01-2	1982	55.00	1982/88	Skrobek	6
Byj 91	A Funny Face From Outer Space *Boy astronaut & alien*	4 7/8"	5297	10091-01-3	1982	65.00	1982/88	Skrobek	6
Byj 92	Dear Sirs *Secretary taking dictation*	5"	5298	10092-01-3	1982	40.00	1982/88	Skrobek	6
Byj 93	Yeah Team *Boy & girl in blanket*	4 5/8"	5307	10093-01-0	1982	65.00	1982/88	Skrobek	6
Byj 94	Not Yet A Vet (Clinic) *Girl tending cat & dog*	4 1/2"	5309	10094-01-2	1982	65.00	1982/88	Skrobek	6
Byj 95	Bedtime Boy (Brown) *Boy kneeling in prayer*	4 1/4"	5404	10095-01-6	1984	26.00	1984/88	Skrobek	6
Byj 96	Bedtime Girl (Brown) *Girl kneeling in prayer*	4"	5405	10096-01-4	1984	26.00	1984/88	Skrobek	6
Byj 97	Sweet Snacks (Blonde) *Girl eating from jam jar*	4 1/4"	5407	10097-01-0	1984	40.00	1984/88	Skrobek	6
Byj 98	All Gone (Brown) *Girl eating from spoon*	3 3/4"	5406	10098-01-2	1984	42.00	1984/88	Skrobek	6

ITEM DESCRIPTION		SIZE	U.S. No.	MOLD No.	MOLD DATE	INITIAL PRICE	INTRO /RETIRE	SCULPTOR	KNOWN TDM'S
Byj 99	Sharing Secrets (Blonde) *Boy talking to duck*	5 1/2"	5408	10099-01-8	1984	44.00	1984/88	Skrobek	6
Byj 100	Farm Friends (Brown) *Girl with flowers & lamb*	4 7/8"	5409	10100-01-4	1984	46.00	1984/88	Skrobek	6
Byj 101	Come Along (Blonde) *Boy hiker*	3 7/8"	5411	10101-01-2	1985	47.50	1985/88	Skrobek	6
Byj 102	Please Wait (Blonde) *Girl hiker sitting on rock*	3 1/8"	5412	10102-01-0	1985	47.50	1985/88	Skrobek	6
Byj 103	Staying Fit (Always Fit) *Boy jogger*	3 3/4"	5361	10103-01-3	1985	45.00	1985/88	Skrobek	6
Byj 104	Almost There (Staying Fit) *Girl jogger*	3 3/4"	5362	10104-01-6	1985	45.00	1985/88	Skrobek	6
Byj 105	The Collector (Figurine Collector) *Girl arranging her dolls*	3 7/8"	5363	10105-01-3	1985	64.00	1985/88	Skrobek	6
Byj 106	The Practice *Girl playing piano*	4 1/8"	5364	10106-01-1	1985	64.00	1985/88	Skrobek	6
Byj 107	Shall We Dance *Girl dancing with Teddy bear*	4 1/8"	5365	10107-12-1	1986	72.50	1986/88	Skrobek	6
Byj 108	Greetings *Angel holding greetings banner*	4 1/2"	5366	10108-12-1	1986	55.00	1986/88	Skrobek	6
Byj 109	A Special Friend *Black angel & kitten on cloud*	4 1/4"	5367	10109-10	1986	55.00	1986/88	Skrobek	6
Byj 110	Communion *Girl in white dress & candle*	4 3/4"		10110-01				Skrobek	Prototype

The 1984 Goebel Retail Price Guide lists Byj 61, 63, 67 and 69 as brown hair. No mention of the Redheads in this guide. In appearance, the figurines really appear to have blonde hair not brown although I have seen figurines in this group with brown hair. A puzzle!

Occasionally a figurine is known by two different names. Where this has occurred the second name appears in parenthesis following the first name. Following each description is a brief description of each item to make identification easier if the name tag is missing.

MUSIC BOXES

ITEM	DESCRIPTION	MOLD NUMBER	INITIAL PRICE	TUNE
Byj 58M	Rock-A-Bye-Baby	10058-01-0	$32.00	Rock-A-Bye-Baby
Byj 60M	Skater's Waltz	10060-01-0	$46.00	Skater's Waltz
Byj 64M	Love Bugs	10064-21-0	$80.00	A Time To Remember

The music box program met with apparent success as they were introduced in 1968 and continued in the line until 1988. Nevertheless, today, they are very scarce items and difficult to locate.

LAMPS

ITEM	DESCRIPTION	PRICE	INITIAL
Byj 42L	Evening Prayer Night Lampwith Byj 38 (Girl With Doll Kneeling In Prayer)		
Byj 70L	Birch Tree Trunk with Byj 6 (A Young Man's Fancy)		Prototype only
Byj71L	Birch Tree Trunk With Byj 10 (Springtime)		Prototype only

The lamp program was not as successful as had been forecast and the program had a very short production period. Actually, the Byj 70 and 71 lamps never made it into regular production as they were made in prototype form only.

1994 LINE ADDITIONS

1994 saw the introduction by the Goebel Porzellanfabrik of a new line based on the artwork of Charlot Byj. The new series is known as "Little Sentiments," is packaged with 10 items to the dealer with each item being in a triangular box and was made in Thailand. Include with each package is a matching greeting card with special messages in several different languages. Figures included are: 3 Redheads, 2 Blondes, 4 blacks and a double figure with a Redhead and a Blonde. Each item was designed to retail for approximately $30.00. The quality of the figurines produced in Thailand is not what we normally expect from W. Goebel Porzellanfabrik.

ITEM NUMBER	DESCRIPTION	SIZE	MOLD
BNR 1	Purfect Friend	4 1/2"	10-113-01-7
	Black girl holding kitten		
BNR 2	You Are Special	4 7/8"	10-114-01-5
	Black girl sitting holding doll		
BNR 3	Praises For You	4 3/4"	10-112-01-9
	Black girl singing from song book		
BNR 4	You're A Perfect Pair	4 3/8"	10-111-01-1
	Redheaded girl & blonde boy on four wheel cart		
BNR 5	What A Knockout	5 1/8"	10-115-01-2
	Redheaded boy with boxing gloves		
BNR 6	In Your Honor	5 1/2"	10-119-01-4
	Blonde boy taking a bow		
BNR 7	You Are Sweet	5 1/8"	10-117-01-8
	Blonde boy with candy box under arm		
BNR 8	Wishing You Sunny Days	5 3/4"	10-118-01-6
	Black girl in yellow raincoat & hat		
BNR 9	Flowers For You	5 1/2"	10-120-01-2
	Redheaded girl holding bouquet of flowers		
BNR 10	Just In Time	4 3/4"	10-116-01-0
	Redheaded boy in towel with envelope in hand		

CHARLOT BYJ ANNUAL
BABY ORNAMENTS

9201	Baby in stocking	(1986)	48-268-01-5	$18.00	Skrobek	6
9202	Baby in snow dress	(1987)	48-270-01-1	$20.00	Skrobek	6
9203	Child in stocking	(1988)	48-269-01-3	$27.00	Skrobek	6
9204	Baby in boot	(1989)	48-271-01-9	????	Skrobek	6
101060	Baby in sled	(1990)	48-273-01-5	$30.00	Skrobek	6
101061	Baby in moon	(1991)	48-272-01-7	$35.00	Skrobek	6

CHARLOT BYJ ANNUAL
CHRISTMAS ORNAMENTS (BELLS)

9101	St. Lucia as small bell	(1986)	44-500-01-5	$18.00	Skrobek	6
9102	Boy as angel holding star bell	(1987)	44-501-01-3	$20.00	Skrobek	6
9103	Angel with music book bell	(1988)	44-502-01-1	$22.50	Skrobek	6
9104	Girl angel holding candle bell	(1989)	44-503-01-9	$22.50	Skrobek	6

Each Plate is 8 1/2". in diameter with the 1973 and 1974 plates boxed in blue boxes while the 1975, 1976 and 1977 are boxed in orange boxes. The pewter plate is boxed in a white chipboard box with black descriptive printing.

1973 Annual Plate	8 1/2"	701	52-701-01-8	$21.00	6
1974 Annual Plate	8 1/2"	703	52-703-01-4	$29.50	6
1975 Annual Plate	8 1/2"	705	52-705-01-9	$29.50	6
1976 Annual Plate	8 1/2"	706	52-706-01-7	$29.50	6
1977 Annual Plate	8 1/2"	707	52-707-01-5	$29.50	6
1979 Pewter Plate	9"	30501	?		6

CALENDARS

January	Byj 26 Good News	July	Byj 57 Madonna Of The Doves
February	Byj 2 Roving Eye	August	Byj 78 Lazy Days
March	Byj 24 Daisies Won't Tell	September	Byj 19 Spellbound
April	Byj 46 The Way To Pray	October	Byj 52 Skater's Waltz
May	Byj 6 A Young Man's Fancy	November	Byj 8 O'Hair For President
June	Byj 10 Springtime	December	Byj 56 Her Shining Hour

Goebel Porzellanfabrik published a calendar featuring the Redhead and Blonde series designed by Charlot Byj for only one year, that being 1980. The firm had a tradition of publishing calendars for the Hummel series dating back to 1957 so this was a natural line extension which lasted only one year. Each month featured a different figurine.

CHARLOT BYJ DOLLS

ITEM	NAME	SIZE	GERMAN PRICE (DM)	U.S. PRICE ($)
Byj 2901A	Raggy Muffin (Trine)	24cm	24.50	55.00
Byj 2901B	Pizza			
Byj 2901C	Reike			
Byj 2901D	Jette			
Byj 2901E	Mary	26cm	24.50	55.00
Byj 2902A	Shabby O'Hair (Stups)	26 cm	21.50	55.00
Byj 2905A	Puffy			
Byj 2906A	Stuffy			
Byj 2906B	Perri	26cm	21.50	
Byj 2907	Matz			
Byj 2908A	Scarlet O'Hair (Fratz)	23cm	16.50	55.00
Byj 2908B	Lucky	8.23cm	16.50	
Byj 2909A	Trampy	23cm	8.90	
Byj 2910A	Tim	17cm	8.90	
Byj 2910B	Topsy	17cm	8.90	
Byj 2911A	Ilka	23cm	14.75	
Byj 2911B	Ina	23cm	14.75	
Byj 2911C	Inka	23cm	14.75	
Byj 2911D	Iris	23cm	14.75	
Byj 2912A	Sigi	17cm	16.50	
Byj 2912B	Thilo	17cm	16.50	
Byj 2913A	Hexi	17cm	16.50	
Byj 2913B	Tina	17cm	16.50	
Byj 2914/1/A	Babe	15cm	8.75	
Byj 2914/2/B	Balla	15cm	8.75	
Byj 2914/1/C	Berit	15cm	8.75	
Byj 2914/2/D	Ben	15cm	8.75	
Byj 2914/2/K	Gesa	15cm	8.75	
Byj 2914/2/I	Gitta	15cm	8.75	
Byj 2914/2/M	Gunda	15cm	8.75	
Byj 2915	Vagabond	22cm	24.50	
Byj 2916/M	Baby		9.80	
Byj 2916/N	Baby		9.80	
Byj 2916/1/R	Baby		9.80	
Byj 2916/1/S	Baby		9.80	
Byj 2917/A	Moony	17cm	8.50	
Byj 2917/B	Moony	17cm	8.50	
Byj 2917/C	Moony	17cm	8.50	
Byj 2917/D	Moony	17cm	8.50	
Byj 2917/E	Moony	17cm	8.50	
00 102	Berni	15cm	8.50	
00 103	Betti	15cm	8.50	
00 116	Jimmy	23cm	8.50	
00 117	Nelly	23cm	16.50	
10 007	Sunny	23cm	16.50	
10 008	Wooly	23cm	19.50	
01 025	Hein	26cm	22.50	
030	Fratz	23cm	24.50	
031	Lucky	23cm	19.50	
032	Sunny	23cm	19.50	
033	Wolly	23cm	19.50	
054	Topsy	17cm	22.50	
055	Tim	17cm	10.50	
00 144	Dirndel		10.50	
00 145	Bub			
00 138	Cowgirl			
00 139	Cowboy			
00 142	Indianerin (Girl)			
00 143	Indianer (Boy)			

ART PRINTS

A bit of background helps understand the succession of firms printing and distributing art prints, greeting cards and other printed items. Dr. Herbert Dubler incorporated the firm "Herbert Dubler, Inc." in 1934 in New York. As such, the firm imported products from the publishing house "Ars Sacra Joseph Mueller Munich." Dr. Dubler was the son-in-law of Joseph Mueller. Herbert Dubler, Inc. was renamed in 1947 "Crestwick, Inc.," taking the name, of the then president, Alfred E. Wick. W. Goebel Porzellanfabrik purchased Crestwick, Inc. in 1956 and the firm became known as "Hummelwerk, Inc." which later was changed to "Goebel United States."

The firm(s) published and or distributed beautifully colored prints, most of which were 13" x 17". format. Later, smaller 8" x 10". prints were issued of some of the same subjects. The following list was taken from an undated "Crestwick Presents" catalogue. All most all of these prints were, in reality, studies that ultimately became Charlot Byj Goebel figurines. Many of the larger prints are marked "Pub. & Copyright by Ars Sacra. Herbert Dubler NY, NY 1947." "Ars" is the Latin word for art.

PRINT NUMBER	TITLE	DESCRIPTION	COMMENT
810	Helping Herself	Blonde girl	Girl reaching into jar. Study for Byj 98.
853	Amen	Blonde girl - brown hair boy	Kneeling in prayer
901	A Child's Prayer	Blonde girl	Study for Byj 17
902	Sitting Pretty	Blonde girl	Study for Byj 12
903	A Stitch In Time	Girl/black hair	Sitting with sewing basket darning a sock
904	Stolen Kiss	Blonde girl/ Red hair boy	Study for Byj 18
905	Washboard Blues	Black girl angel	Sitting with washboard on cloud. Study for Byj 109
906	City Slicker	Black boy	Walking in yellow rain suit with umbrella
907	Slick Chick	Black girl	Walking in yellow rain cape with umbrella
908	Serenade	Redheaded boy	Study for Byj 85
909	The Offering	Blonde girl & shrine	Study for Byj 54/59
912	Bless Us All	Blonde boy	Study for Byj 16
913	Freckle Face	Redheaded boy	Freckle face boy in straw hat & overalls
914	Rosy Cheeks	Blonde girl	Study for Byj 12
915	Tete-a-Tete	Blonde boy	Study for Byj 99
916	Vanity	Blonde girl	Girl looking in mirror trying on hat
917	Fairy Tales	Redheaded girl	Study for Byj 86
918	Puttering Around	Blonde boy	Squatting down playing in mud & water
919	Mischievous	Redheaded girl	Sitting - kitten playing with ribbon
920	Towhead	Blonde boy	In overalls playing with three baby chicks
922	Scrub Team	Black girl	Girl with pail scrubbing floor - kittens in bubbles
923	Suds "n Duds	Black girl	Washing clothes in washtub. Two kittens
924	Grace Before Meals	Blonde girl	Sitting at table saying grace

PRINT NUMBER	TITLE	DESCRIPTION	COMMENT
925	Grace After Meals	Brunette boy	With napkin around neck saying grace
926	Starlet	Dark hair	Angel sleeping on cloud
927	Starling	Redheaded boy	Study for Byj 15
928	Bonny	Blonde girl	Sweet girl with bonnet on head
929	Sleepyhead	Blonde boy	Study for Byj 11
930	Adoration	Dark hair	Angel kissing baby in manger
951	Budding Genius	Redheaded girl	Study for Byj 19
952	Greedy Petey	Redheaded boy	Sitting eating bread/jelly, candy in back pocket & cake on ground
	Tender Shepherd		Study for Byj 55

HISTORIC PRICING INFORMATION

The pricing information that follows is based on original retail price guides as published by W. Goebel Porzellanfabrik, Germany. Pricing information is missing for the years of 1957, 1959, 1960, 1961, 1962, 1963, 1964, 1965, 1966, 1967, 1968, 1970, 1971, 1985 and 1989. If you have complete Goebel Retail Price Guides for any of these years please contact me. My address may be found in the front of this book in the copyright data section.

The purpose of providing this information is to give you an idea, not only of the pricing, but when items were introduced and discontinued from the line. Although some figurines may have been produced for only one or two years they may have been listed in the Goebel Retail Price Guide for several years until the inventory in the distribution system had been sold. By carefully studying the data in this section and the data in the Quick List Section pertaining to the dates of production and retirement, you can determine which pieces are rare even though they were regular items in the line. A little hint – look for those items which were produced for only one or two years.

One further comment, if no price appears in a square in this pricing history section it means that there was no price listed in the Goebel Retail Price Guide and therefore the figurine was apparently not available for that year.

BYJ PRICING HISTORY, 1957-1966

Byj #	Description	1957	1958	1959	1960	1961	1962	1963	1964	1965	1966
1	Strike		6.00								
2	The Roving Eye		6.00								
3	Oops		8.00								
4	Little Miss Coy		6.00								
5	Shear Nonsense		10.00								
6	A Young Man's Fancy		10.00								
7	Atta Boy		6.50								
8	O'Hair For President		6.00								
9	E-ee-eek		8.00								
10	Springtime		7.50								
11	Sleepyhead										
12	Sitting Pretty										
13	Blank number only										
14	Blank number only										
15	Starling (Plaque)										
16	Bless Us All										
17	A Child's Prayer										
18	The Stolen Kiss		13.00								
19	Spellbound		12.00								
20	Forbidden Fruit		7.00								
21	Moonlight Sonata Wall Plaque										
22	Off Key		7.50								
23	The Kibitzer		7.50								
24	Daisies Won't Tell		6.00								
25	Putting On The Dog		9.00								
26	Good News		6.00								
27	Plenty Of Nothing		5.50								
28	Gangway		8.50								
29	Calorie Counter – Plaque										

Byj #	Description	1957	1958	1959	1960	1961	1962	1963	1964	1965	1966
30	Girl – muff/tray – salt & pep.										
31	Gingerbread boy & girl s & p										
32	Gingerbread man & woman										
33	Umbrella candy dish										
34	Old Man Street Cleaner										
35	Spring Cleaning										
36	Mother Embracing Child										
37	Rock-A-Bye-Baby										
38	Evening Prayer										
39	Super Service			9.00							
40	Guess Who		8.50								
44	Lucky Day								5.50		
45	Dropping In								6.00		
46	The Way To Pray										
47	Display Plaque										4.00
48	Copper Topper										
49	Trim Lass										
50	Cheer Up										
51	Let It Rain										
52	Skater's Waltz										
53	Little Shopper										
55	Tender Shepherd										
56	Her Shining Hour										
57	Madonna of The Doves										
59	Little Prayers Are Best										
61	First Degree										
62	Swinger										
63	The Nurse										
64	Love Bugs										
65	Bongo Beat										
66	Baby Sitter										
67	Trouble Shooter										
68	Say A-a-aah										
69	Bachelor Degree										
70	Lamp with Byj #6 – Prototype										
71	Lamp with Byj #10 Prototype										
72	Damper On The Camper										
73	Heads Or Tails										
74	Wash Day										
75	Sea Breeze										
76	Barbeque										
77	1-2 Ski Doo										
78	Lazy Day										
79	Camera Shy										
80	Prototype only										
81	Prototype only										
82	Prototype only										
83	Fore										
84	Bird Watcher										
85	Captive Audience										
86	Once Upon A Time										
87	Four Letter Word For Ouch										
88	Something Tells Me										
89	Yech										
90	Nothing Beats A Pizza										
91	A Funny Face From Outer										
92	Dear Sirs										
93	Yeah Team										
94	Not Yet A Vet										
95	Bedtime Boy										
96	Bedtime Girl										
97	All Gone										
98	Sweet Snacks										
99	Sharing Secrets										
100	Farm Friends										
101	Come Along										
102	Please Wait										
103	Staying Fit										
104	Almost There										
105	The Collector										

Byj #	Description	1957	1958	1959	1960	1961	1962	1963	1964	1965	1966
106	The Practice										
107	Shall We Dance										
108	Greetings										
109	A Special Friend										
110	Communion										
1973	Plates										
1974	Plates										
1975	Plates										
1976	Plates										
1977	Plates										
	Pewter Plate										

BYJ PRICING HISTORY, 1967-1976

Byj #	Description	1967	1968	1969	1970	1971	1972	1973	1974	1975	1976
1	Strike			6.50			12.00	12.50	15.00	16.50	18.00
2	The Roving Eye			6.50			10.00	10.50	13.00	15.00	16.50
3	Oops			8.50			14.00	15.00	18.50	20.50	24.00
4	Little Miss Coy			6.50			11.00	11.50	14.00	15.50	15.50
5	Shear Nonsense			10.50			18.00	19.00	23.00	25.50	30.00
6	A Young Man's Fancy			10.50			20.00	21.00	25.50	28.00	32.00
7	Atta Boy			7.00			13.00	14.00	17.00	18.50	18.50
8	O'Hair For President			6.50			13.00	14.00	17.00	18.50	18.50
9	E-ee-eek			8.50			15.50	16.50	20.00	22.00	24.00
10	Springtime			8.00			15.50	16.50	20.00	22.00	25.00
11	Sleepyhead			8.50			14.50	15.00	18.50	20.50	20.50
12	Sitting Pretty			9.50			20.00	21.00	25.50	28.00	30.00
13	Blank number only										
14	Blank number only										
15	Starling (Plaque)										
16	Bless Us All			6.50			12.00	12.50	15.00	16.50	16.50
17	A Child's Prayer			6.50			12.00	12.50	15.00	16.50	16.50
18	The Stolen Kiss			13.50			24.00	25.00	30.50	33.50	40.00
19	Spellbound			12.50			22.00	23.00	27.50	30.00	30.00
20	Forbidden Fruit			7.50			13.00	14.00	17.00	18.50	18.50
21	Moonlight Sonata Wall Plaque										
22	Off Key			8.00			14.50	15.00	18.50	20.50	22.00
23	The Kibitzer			8.00			14.50	15.00	18.50	20.50	22.00
24	Daisies Won't Tell			6.50			13.00	14.00	17.00	18.50	18.50
25	Putting On The Dog			9.50			18.00	19.00	23.00	25.50	25.50
26	Good News			6.50			12.00	12.50	15.00	16.50	18.00
27	Plenty Of Nothing			6.00			11.00	11.50	14.00	16.50	16.50
28	Gangway			9.00			15.50	16.50	20.00	25.00	25.00
29	Calorie Counter – Plaque										
30	Girl – muff/tray – salt & pep.										
31	Gingerbread boy & girl s & p										
32	Gingerbread man & woman										
33	Umbrella candy dish										
34	Old Man Street Cleaner										
35	Spring Cleaning										
36	Mother Embracing Child			12.50			24.00	25.00	30.50	33.50	33.50
37	Rock-A-Bye-Baby			8.00			15.00	16.50	20.00	22.00	22.00
38	Evening Prayer			8.50			15.00	16.50	20.00	22.00	22.00
39	Super Service			9.50			18.00	19.00	28.50	31.50	31.50
40	Guess Who			9.00			18.00	19.00	28.50	31.50	31.50
44	Lucky Day			6.00			12.00	12.50	15.00	16.50	16.50
45	Dropping In			6.50			13.00	14.00	17.00	18.50	18.50
46	The Way To Pray			9.00			15.50	16.50	20.00	22.00	24.00
47	Display Plaque			4.50			7.50	8.00	10.00	11.00	11.00
48	Copper Topper	10.00		9.50			14.50	15.00	18.50	20.50	20.50
49	Trim Lass	14.00		14.00			20.00	21.00	25.50	28.00	28.00
50	Cheer Up	8.00		8.50			14.50	15.00	18.50	20.50	20.50
51	Let It Rain	26.00		26.00			42.00	44.00	53.00	58.50	58.50
52	Skater's Waltz	15.00		14.00			20.00	21.00	25.50	28.00	30.00
53	Little Shopper	13.00		13.00			20.00	21.00	25.50	28.00	30.00
54	Little Prayers Are Best	13.00									
55	Tender Shepherd			8.50			15.00	16.00	19.50		
56	Her Shining Hour			14.00			20.00	21.00	25.50	28.00	28.00

Byj #	Description	1967	1968	1969	1970	1971	1972	1973	1974	1975	1976
57	Madonna of The Doves			26.00			42.00	44.00	53.00	90.00	90.00
58M	Rock-A-Bye (Music Box)			22.00			30.00	32.00		50.00	
59	Little Prayers Are Best			12.00			18.00	19.00	22.50	22.50	25.50
60M	Skater's Waltz (Music Box)			25.00			44.00	46.00		60.00	
61	First Degree				18.00		18.00	19.00	23.00	22.50	25.50
62	Swinger				15.00		18.00	19.00	23.00	22.50	25.50
63	The Nurse				13.00		15.50	16.50	20.00	22.00	22.00
64	Love Bugs						38.00	40.00	48.50	55.00	55.00
64M	Love Bugs (Music Box)						50.00	52.00		70.00	
65	Bongo Beat				18.50		22.00	23.00	27.50	30.00	30.00
66	Baby Sitter				28.00		28.00	29.50	36.00	39.50	39.50
67	Trouble Shooter				13.00		15.50	16.50	20.00	22.00	22.00
68	Say A-a-aah				19.00		19.00	20.00	24.00	26.50	26.50
69	Bachelor Degree				18.00		18.00	19.00	23.00	25.50	25.50
70	Lamp with Byj #6 – Prototype										
71	Lamp with Byj #10 Prototype										
72	Damper On The Camper										
73	Heads Or Tails										
74	Wash Day									55.00	55.00
75	Sea Breeze										
76	Barbeque									55.00	55.00
77	1-2 Ski Doo										
78	Lazy Day									55.00	55.00
79	Camera Shy									48.00	48.00
80	Prototype only										
81	Prototype only										
82	Prototype only										
83	Fore									48.00	48.00
84	Bird Watcher									48.00	48.00
85	Captive Audience										
86	Once Upon A Time										
87	Four Letter Word For Ouch										
88	Something Tells Me										
89	Yech										
90	Nothing Beats A Pizza										
91	A Funny Face From Outer										
92	Dear Sirs										
93	Yeah Team										
94	Not Yet A Vet										
95	Bedtime Boy										
96	Bedtime Girl										
97	All Gone										
98	Sweet Snacks										
99	Sharing Secrets										
100	Farm Friends										
101	Come Along										
102	Please Wait										
103	Staying Fit										
104	Almost There										
105	The Collector										
106	The Practice										
107	Shall We Dance										
108	Greetings										
109	A Special Friend										
110	Communion										
1973	Plates							16.50		18.00	18.00
1974	Plates								22.00	24.00	24.00
1975	Plates									25.00	25.00
1976	Plates										25.00
1977	Plates										
	Pewter Plate										49.00

BYJ PRICING HISTORY, 1977-1985

Byj #	Description	1977	1978	1979	1980	1981	1982	1983	1984	1985
1	Strike	21.00	27.00	30.00	36.00	36.00	36.00	36.00	36.00	
2	The Roving Eye	20.00	27.00	31.00	37.50	37.50	37.50	37.50	37.50	
3	Oops	28.00	36.00	42.00	50.00	50.00	50.00	50.00	50.00	
4	Little Miss Coy	17.50	24.00	28.00	32.50	33.00	33.00	33.00	33.00	

Byj #	Description	1977	1978	1979	1980	1981	1982	1983	1984	1985
5	Shear Nonsense	35.00	46.00	53.00	65.00	65.00	65.00	65.00	65.00	
6	A Young Man's Fancy	39.00	51.00	58.00	70.00	70.00	70.00	70.00	70.00	
7	Atta Boy	25.00	32.00	37.00	42.00	42.00	42.00	42.00	42.00	
8	O'Hair For President	25.00	32.00	38.00	45.00	45.00	45.00	45.00	45.00	
9	E-ee-eek	30.00	39.00	48.00	53.00	53.00	53.00	53.00	53.00	
10	Springtime	27.50	37.00	48.00	50.00	50.00	50.00	50.00	50.00	
11	Sleepyhead	25.00	32.00	37.00	45.00	45.00	45.00	45.00	45.00	
12	Sitting Pretty	33.00	48.00	53.00	64.00	64.00	64.00	64.00	64.00	
13	Blank number only									
14	Blank number only									
15	Starling (Plaque)									
16	Bless Us All	20.00	29.00	32.00	37.50	37.50	37.50	37.50	37.50	
17	A Child's Prayer	20.00	29.00	32.00	37.50	37.50	37.50	37.50	37.50	
18	The Stolen Kiss	45.00	52.00							
19	Spellbound	37.00	54.00	60.00	70.00	70.00	70.00	70.00	70.00	
20	Forbidden Fruit	22.00	27.50							
21	Moonlight Sonata Wall Plaque									
22	Off Key	27.00	35.00	42.00	48.00	48.00	48.00	48.00	48.00	
23	The Kibitzer	27.00	35.00	42.00	48.00	48.00	48.00	48.00	48.00	
24	Daisies Won't Tell	22.00	31.00	35.50	41.00	42.00	42.00	42.00	42.00	
25	Putting On The Dog	30.00	43.00	49.00	57.00	60.00	60.00	60.00	60.00	
26	Good News	22.00	29.00	33.00	37.50	37.50	37.50	37.50	37.50	
27	Plenty Of Nothing	17.50	23.00	26.50	30.00	30.00	30.00	30.00	30.00	
28	Gangway	30.00	40.00	46.00	55.00	55.00	55.00	55.00	55.00	
29	Calorie Counter – Plaque									
30	Girl – muff/tray – salt & pep.									
31	Gingerbread boy & girl s & p									
32	Gingerbread man & woman									
33	Umbrella candy dish									
34	Old Man Street Cleaner									
35	Spring Cleaning									
36	Mother Embracing Child	40.00	60.00	66.00	76.00	80.00	80.00	80.00	80.00	
37	Rock-A-Bye-Baby	27.00	40.00	43.00	48.00	50.00	50.00	50.00	50.00	
38	Evening Prayer	27.00	40.00	43.00	50.00	50.00	50.00	50.00	50.00	
39	Super Service	35.00	44.00							
40	Guess Who	35.00	50.00							
44	Lucky Day	20.00	30.00	32.50	37.00	37.00	37.00	37.00	37.50	
45	Dropping In	22.00	31.00	34.50	41.00	43.00	43.00	43.00	43.00	
46	The Way To Pray	28.00	37.00	43.00	52.00	55.00	55.00	55.00	55.00	
47	Display Plaque	12.00	15.00	20.00	22.00	22.00	22.00	22.00	22.00	
48	Copper Topper	25.00	32.00	36.00	42.00	44.00	44.00	44.00	44.00	
49	Trim Lass	34.00	39.50							
50	Cheer Up	23.00	29.00	34.00	38.00	40.00	40.00	40.00	40.00	
51	Let It Rain	70.00	95.00	104.00	120.00	125.00	125.00	125.00	125.00	
52	Skater's Waltz	35.00	45.00		55.00	60.00	60.00	60.00	60.00	
53	Little Shopper	35.00	40.50							
54	Little Prayers Are Best									
55	Tender Shepherd									
56	Her Shining Hour	34.00		55.00	65.00	70.00	70.00	70.00	70.00	
57	Madonna of The Doves	95.00	124.00	136.00	136.00	145.00	145.00	145.00	145.00	
58M	Rock-A-Bye (Music Box)	65.00		92.00	92.00			95.00	95.00	
59	Little Prayers Are Best	30.00	39.00	45.00	52.00	55.00	55.00	55.00	55.00	
60M	Skater's Waltz (Music Box)	70.00								
61	First Degree (Red Hair)	30.00	39.00	45.00	52.00	52.00	52.00	52.00	52.00	
61	First Degree (Brown Hair)								49.00	
62	Swinger	30.00	35.00	50.00	55.00	55.00	55.00	55.00	55.00	
63	The Nurse (Red Hair)	27.00	35.00	42.00	50.00	52.50	52.50	52.50	52.50	
63	The Nurse (Brown Hair)								49.00	
64	Love Bugs	65.00	76.00							
64M	Love Bugs (Music Box)	100.00								
65	Bongo Beat	35.00	44.00	60.00	65.00					
66	Baby Sitter	43.00	56.00	70.00	80.00	84.00	84.00	84.00	84.00	
67	Trouble Shooter	27.00	35.00	42.00	47.00	49.50	49.50	49.50	49.50	
67	This Won't Hurt (Blonde Hair)									
68	Say A-a-aah	30.00	39.00	52.00	60.00	60.00	60.00	60.00	60.00	
69	Bachelor Degree (Red Hair)	30.00	39.00	50.00	55.00	55.00	55.00	55.00	55.00	
69	Bachelor Degree (Brown Hair)								49.00	
70	Lamp with Byj #6 – Prototype									
71	Lamp with Byj #10 Prototype									
72	Damper On The Camper							75.00	75.00	75.00

Byj #	Description	1977	1978	1979	1980	1981	1982	1983	1984	1985
73	Heads Or Tails						60.00	60.00	60.00	
74	Wash Day	60.00	78.00	87.00	100.00	100.00	100.00	100.00	100.00	
75	Sea Breeze						65.00	65.00	65.00	
76	Barbeque	60.00	78.00	87.00	100.00	100.00	100.00	100.00	100.00	
77	1-2 Ski Doo						75.00	75.00	75.00	
78	Lazy Day	60.00	78.00	87.00	100.00	100.00	100.00	100.00	100.00	
79	Camera Shy	60.00	78.00	87.00	85.00	90.00	90.00	90.00	90.00	
80	Prototype only									
81	Prototype only									
82	Prototype only									
83	Fore	50.00	65.00	78.00	85.00	90.00	90.00	90.00	90.00	
84	Bird Watcher	50.00	65.00	78.00	85.00	90.00	90.00	90.00	90.00	
85	Captive Audience									
86	Once Upon A Time									
87	Four Letter Word For Ouch							40.00	40.00	
88	Something Tells Me							40.00	40.00	
89	Yech									
90	Nothing Beats A Pizza							55.00	55.00	
91	A Funny Face From Outer							65.00	65.00	
92	Dear Sirs							40.00	40.00	
93	Yeah Team									
94	Not Yet A Vet									
95	Bedtime Boy									
96	Bedtime Girl									
97	All Gone									
98	Sweet Snacks									
99	Sharing Secrets									
100	Farm Friends									
101	Come Along									
102	Please Walt									
103	Staying Fit									
104	Almost There									
105	The Collector									
106	The Practice									
107	Shall We Dance									
108	Greetings									
109	A Special Friend									
110	Communion									
1973	Plates	18.00	21.00							
1974	Plates	24.00	29.50	29.50	30.00					
1975	Plates	25.00	29.00	29.50	30.00					
1976	Plates	25.00	29.50	29.50	30.00					
1977	Plates	25.00	24.50	29.50	30.00					
	Pewter Plate	49.00								

BYJ PRICING HISTORY, 1986-1989

Byj #	Description	1986	1987	1988	1989
1	Strike				
2	The Roving Eye	44.00			
3	Oops	58.00	68.00	68.00	
4	Little Miss Coy	38.00	45.00	45.00	
5	Shear Nonsense	75.00			
6	A Young Man's Fancy	80.00	92.00	92.00	
7	Atta Boy				
8	O'Hair For President				
9	E-ee-eek	60.00			
10	Springtime				
11	Sleepyhead				
12	Sitting Pretty				
13	Blank number only				
14	Blank number only				
15	Starling (Plaque)				
16	Bless Us All	44.00	50.00	50.00	
17	A Child's Prayer	44.00			
18	The Stolen Kiss				
19	Spellbound	80.00			
20	Forbidden Fruit				
21	Moonlight Sonata Wall Plaque				

Byj #	Description	1986	1987	1988	1989
22	Off Key				
23	The Kibitzer				
24	Daisies Won't Tell				
25	Putting On The Dog				
26	Good News	44.00	50.00	50.00	
27	Plenty Of Nothing				
28	Gangway				
29	Calorie Counter – Plaque				
30	Girl – muff/tray – salt & pep.				
31	Gingerbread boy & girl s & p				
32	Gingerbread man & woman				
33	Umbrella candy dish				
34	Old Man Street Cleaner				
35	Spring Cleaning				
36	Mother Embracing Child	95.00			
37	Rock-A-Bye-Baby	58.00	68.00	68.00	50.00
38	Evening Prayer	58.00			
39	Super Service				
40	Guess Who				
44	Lucky Day				
45	Dropping In	48.00	55.00	55.00	
46	The Way To Pray	66.00			50.00
47	Display Plaque	25.00	30.00	30.00	
48	Copper Topper				
49	Trim Lass				
50	Cheer Up	48.00	55.00	55.00	
51	Let It Rain	145.00	160.00	160.00	
52	Skater's Waltz	70.00			
53	Little Shopper				
55	Tender Shepherd				
56	Her Shining Hour	80.00			
57	Madonna of The Doves	169.00	185.00	185.00	185.00
58M	Rock-A-Bye (Music Box)				
59	Little Prayers Are Best	58.00			
60M	Skater's Waltz (Music Box)				
61	First Degree (Red Hair)				
61	First Degree (Brown Hair)	58.00	68.00	68.00	
62	Swinger				
63	The Nurse (Red Hair)	58.00	68.00	68.00	
63	The Nurse (Brown Hair)	58.00	68.00	68.00	
64	Love Bugs				
64M	Love Bugs (Music Box)				
65	Bongo Beat				
66	Baby Sitter				
67	Trouble Shooter (Red Hair)	58.00			
67	This Won't Hurt (Blonde Hair)	58.00			
68	Say A-a-aah				
69	Bachelor Degree (Red Hair)				
69	Bachelor Degree (Brn Hair)	50.00	68.00	68.00	
70	Lamp with Byj #6 – Prototype				
71	Lamp with Byj #10 Prototype				
72	Damper On The Camper				
73	Heads Or Tails				
74	Wash Day				
75	Sea Breeze				
76	Barbeque				
77	1-2 Ski Doo				
78	Lazy Day				
79	Camera Shy				
80	Prototype only				
81	Prototype only				
82	Prototype only				
83	Fore				
84	Bird Watcher				
85	Captive Audience	66.00	72.50	72.50	
86	Once Upon A Time	66.00	72.50	72.50	
87	Four Letter Word For Ouch	48.00	55.00	55.00	
88	Something Tells Me	48.00			
89	Yech	66.00			
90	Nothing Beats A Pizza	66.00	72.50	72.50	

Byj #	Description	1986	1987	1988	1989
91	A Funny Face From Outer	75.00			
92	Dear Sirs	48.00	55.00	55.00	
93	Yeah Team	75.00			
94	Not Yet A Vet	75.00	85.00	85.00	
95	Bedtime Boy	35.00			
96	Bedtime Girl	35.00			
97	All Gone	58.00			
98	Sweet Snacks	58.00			
99	Sharing Secrets	58.00			
100	Farm Friends	66.00			
101	Come Along		47.50	47.50	
102	Please Wait		47.50	47.50	
103	Staying Fit		45.00	45.00	
104	Almost There		45.00	45.00	
105	The Collector		64.00	64.00	
106	The Practice		64.00	64.00	
107	Shall We Dance			72.50	
108	Greetings			55.00	
109	A Special Friend			55.00	
110	Communion				
	1986 Santa Lucia Bell	18.00	18.00		
	1986 Baby Ornament	18.00	18.00		
	1987 Baby Snow Ornament		20.00	20.00	
	1987 Christmas Ornament		20.00	20.00	
	1988 Baby's 1st Ornament			22.50	
	1988 Baby's 1st Stocking			27.50	
	1973 Plates				
	1974 Plates				
	1975 Plates				
	1976 Plates				
	1977 Plates				
	Pew Plates				